Why I Help People Take Drugs

Why I Help People Take Drugs

*Reflections of a Christian
Addiction Medicine Physician*

MEERA BAI GROVER

CASCADE *Books* • Eugene, Oregon

WHY I HELP PEOPLE TAKE DRUGS
Reflections of a Christian Addiction Medicine Physician

Copyright © 2024 Meera Bai Grover. All rights reserved. Except for brief quotations in critical publications or reviews, no part of this book may be reproduced in any manner without prior written permission from the publisher. Write: Permissions, Wipf and Stock Publishers, 199 W. 8th Ave., Suite 3, Eugene, OR 97401.

Cascade Books
An Imprint of Wipf and Stock Publishers
199 W. 8th Ave., Suite 3
Eugene, OR 97401

www.wipfandstock.com

PAPERBACK ISBN: 979-8-3852-1002-2
HARDCOVER ISBN: 979-8-3852-1003-9
EBOOK ISBN: 979-8-3852-1004-6

Cataloguing-in-Publication data:

Names: Grover, Meera Bai, author.

Title: Why I help people take drugs : reflections of a Christian addiction medicine physician / Meera Bai Grover.

Description: Eugene, OR : Cascade Books, 2024 | Includes bibliographical references.

Identifiers: ISBN 979-8-3852-1002-2 (paperback) | ISBN 979-8-3852-1003-9 (hardcover) | ISBN 979-8-3852-1004-6 (ebook)

Subjects: LCSH: Harm reduction. | Drug abuse—Prevention. | Drug control—Religious aspects—Christianity.

Classification: HV5801 .G78 2024 (paperback) | HV5801 .G78 (ebook)

08/29/24

All Scripture quotations, unless otherwise indicated, are taken from the Holy Bible, New International Version®, NIV®. Copyright ©1973, 1978, 1984, 2011 by Biblica, Inc.™ Used by permission of Zondervan. All rights reserved worldwide. www.zondervan.com The "NIV" and "New International Version" are trademarks registered in the United States Patent and Trademark Office by Biblica, Inc.™

For Jake and for Alicia

Contents

	Preface	ix
	Introduction	xi
1	Addiction	1
2	Crisis	14
3	Trauma	23
4	Harm Reduction	31
5	Justice	41
6	Treatment	52
7	Bad Medicine	62
8	Dogma	76
9	Neighborhoods	88
10	Free Will	99
11	Judgment	106
12	Personal Change	113
13	Structural Change	119
	Conclusion	124
	Bibliography	127

Preface

FIRST AND FOREMOST, I would like to thank you for reading this book. Countless hours went into writing it as a doctor who worked in hospitals during the COVID-19 pandemic. For that reason alone, I am proud of getting it written. It is my hope that this book will help you understand my perspective as a Christian addiction medicine physician as I tell you stories about my interactions with patients and my own reflections on morality in my work. I truly believe I have the best job in the world, and I hope these stories will show you why.

There is a saying in our field—"nothing about me, without me." Although the stories in this book are my own, they involve my patients. To that end I have asked a handful of people with lived experience to read through my book to help make sure I am representing my patients fairly. I don't think any book about people with a substance use disorder should be published without input from people with a substance use disorder. I have also asked BIPOC friends to read my book to help point out any areas where I have been unintentionally racist. Despite these efforts, I am sure that I have been accidentally offensive in places. It just happens when you're talking about perspectives you don't fully understand. I can never fully understand what it means to be someone who has a substance use disorder or someone of a different ethnicity than me. It doesn't mean I won't keep trying to speak out, just that I will embrace a posture of learning and apologizing as I go.

PREFACE

This book was a group effort—countless hours from several people went into making this book into a reality. My family and friends helped encourage me to write it and provided guidance along the way. I'm grateful to the several physician colleagues and superiors who read drafts at various stages and provided me with guidance. I am also grateful for my nursing, social work, peer support, and pharmacy colleagues who read it and gave me feedback. Physicians are not the backbone of addiction medicine—we always work as a team with other healthcare providers to support our patients. I figured if we are all needed in helping patients at work, we're all needed in helping advocate for patients through this book. And I'm also grateful to the pastors who have read the book to help make sure I do not misrepresent the work of God in the world and by doing so, take his name in vain.

I want to give thanks for the people whose land I write this book on. I write with my feet planted in the traditional territories of the peoples of Treaty 7, which include the Blackfoot Confederacy (comprised of the Siksika, the Piikani, and the Kainai First Nations), the Tsuut'ina First Nation, and the Stoney Nakoda (including Chiniki, Bearspaw, and Goodstoney First Nations), as well as the Métis Nation of Alberta (Districts 5 and 6). It is my belief that wisdom comes from connection with the land and the people who came before me, and I rely on this in the writing of this book.

Finally, I must thank my patients for the privilege of being their physician. I will forever be humbled and in awe of the intimate spaces in my patients' hearts into which I am granted access.

This book does not represent the views of anybody I work for, or any organizations I work with. I have no financial disclosures and no pharmaceutical companies are paying me to espouse their views. This book is instead the work of my own heart over years of contemplation and prayer while serving in this field. It is my hope that as you read this, you will journey alongside me into unexpected places where I have found God at work. May this book be a blessing to you and to those around you.

Introduction

SO THERE I WAS, first day on the job at Insite—Canada's first supervised consumption site for illicit drugs. I had no idea what I'd gotten myself into, and all I knew is that I was way out of my element. As I watched my first patient stumble toward me, I wondered if I had made a big mistake. He was hunched over, stringy hair in patches, sores all over his face, and he did not smell good. I looked to the more experienced staff member by the door, but he was busy.

Insite was a scary place for a middle-class woman, and yet somehow I had found myself there. The main room where I stood nervously was a large open space with several booths along the outer walls, each with a seat facing a wall mirror and a table. A nurse's station along the middle of the back wall had eyes on all the patients, and a table with self-serve injection supplies was available. The waiting room was full of people antsy to get using, sometimes shaking with withdrawal, waiting for their turn. The chill-out room after use had people eating snacks and soaking their feet in warm basins, warming up and chatting with staff once their urgent needs had been met.

As the intoxicated homeless man approached me, I tried to manage my anxiety by quickly running through possible health questions he might ask me and how I would answer. I was determined to remain professional, to show him I cared. Before I could say a word, he'd already started.

"Your eyes are too close together."

My . . . what?

INTRODUCTION

"You heard me. Too close. Don't get me wrong, I would still do you, but it'd cost you more."

Uhhh . . . okay. I'd just gotten insulted and propositioned. He leaned in closer. "Baby, I got moves you ain't never heard of. I'm known for my gumming." Then he grinned widely, revealing rows of gums where teeth should be. A little drool slid down the side of his face. I didn't know whether to be offended or flattered. So much for keeping things professional.

I started laughing, then muffled it, afraid I might have offended my first patient. He laughed too, then high-fived me. "Welcome to Insite. You'll do just fine here."

I suppose I should probably start by telling you a little bit about how I found myself at Insite that day, checking the mirror to see if my eyes really are too close together. (They're not).

Before I do, however, I need to toss in a little disclaimer here. The stories in this book may sometimes be difficult to read, because they are authentic. As I discuss the realities of addiction, the same authenticity that makes some of this book unpleasant is also what makes it an honest search for God. That being said, this is the story of my own journey in learning about the morality of addiction medicine. I don't speak for any of the places I work for. I speak simply as a Christian who above all else is trying her best to figure out how to follow God.

I grew up in a single parent household, with a mother who had been deeply hurt by the culture of her family. I had a difficult childhood full of poverty and abuse. My mother was staunchly atheist, and had brought me up to question religion ferociously, with strong intelligence and a deep mistrust. Despite this, I somehow made friends in high school with people who had different beliefs. One friend in particular was an evangelical Christian, and he took my hatred in with good will. He patiently allowed my criticism of his intellect to wash over him, and he stayed steadfast in his faith. He invited me to church and I went, looking for other ways to put down this religion. Christianity angered me because it brainwashed him and other nice people like him into doing harm in the world.

INTRODUCTION

Instead, at church, I found people with integrity and passion, who genuinely cared about doing what was right. And somehow, God met me there, right where I was at, in all my rage. I want to acknowledge that there are many churches, and many people in churches, who lack integrity. But I had encountered a God who expected it, who could not accept evil, and who loved all people deeply. I found that God loved me regardless of the evil in me, without endorsing it, and without ignoring it. He just stayed with me, seeing all of me, including the worst parts, and still loving me without leaving. Developing a relationship with God was and still is an unbelievable, mystical, hope-filled experience of being entirely seen and entirely loved. This is the experience that I believe God wants for all of us. Somewhere along the way, I found that I had become a Christian. Still, I struggled with the Bible, and the parts of it that did not seem to fit with this God I had learned about.

I decided that I wanted to pursue graduate studies in theology at Regent College on the University of British Columbia campus in Vancouver. I had been baptized into a wonderful church community before eventually, with their blessing, becoming a part of a little Baptist church plant in an inner city neighborhood. Despite getting really great teaching from my church and the many Christians in my life, I wanted a more solid academic foundation into Scripture—could I really believe in the Bible as a true and guiding authority when so many parts seemed so unjust? So, I applied to Regent, and started looking into job opportunities as a nurse in BC. Theological education is expensive, and I had to support myself somehow.

At Regent, I learned how to read the Old Testament and the New Testament, and how to access resources to help me understand the texts. I started seeing the Bible as several books in a library curated by someone I trusted. I learned how to wrestle with the parts of Scripture that I felt were unjust, and I came out of it with a deeper trust that I believed in a God who is wholly good and wholly just. Just as importantly, I learned how to better love all people as made in God's image and deserving of kindness. This passion for the equality of all people came from my study of Scripture combined with regular prayer and a continued relationship with God. I tend to use all of these things when determining right from wrong. These practices helped me to navigate a world where I could not see other visible Christians, a place that I had assumed to be God-forsaken.

When I applied to Regent, I specifically looked in the downtown eastside for nursing work as I figured hey, what better place to contextualize my learning about God than among the most marginalized of our society? "Wait, I thought a doctor wrote this book," you think to yourself. Well, I just so happened to have started my career in addiction medicine as a nurse, so some of these stories are from my nursing career, and some are from my medical one. East Hastings, by the way, is the poorest urban postal code in Canada. HIV rates there have dropped since Insite opened up, but started off a few years before as some of the highest in the world.

I had heard about this place called Insite, and I had mixed feelings about it. All I knew was that it was a place where people could go to shoot up drugs legally and pretty much just act in the most ungodly ways imaginable. It wasn't something I was particularly keen to be involved in, but I knew that I wanted to do something among people who are marginalized. I was a fairly new nurse, and it was important to me to use my skills as best as I could to follow God. So I called up Vancouver Coastal Health and requested to apply for a job at a clinic in the Downtown Eastside. It was then that I found out that all of the nurses at the clinic I was applying to were also cross-trained at Insite. The recruiting officer asked me on the phone if I was okay with working at Insite. The professional in me immediately said yes, but as I hung up, I wondered if I had committed to more than my faith would allow.

As the days leading up to my interview passed, I was consumed with doubts. As a practicing conservative evangelical Christian, was it immoral for me to help people inject drugs? Could I, as a nurse, help somebody find a vein if I knew they were just going to inject drugs into it? Wasn't I enabling them? Shouldn't I instead be telling them about the love of Christ so they can renounce the

INTRODUCTION

drugs and start a completely different life? I could not picture a way in which following Jesus and maintaining integrity as a Christian and a nurse would allow me to work at Insite.

As my interview approached, I didn't know what to do. Thankfully, I learned that Insite is a place where you need to be open. They don't put up with the polite facade that many workplaces require, and instead request that you wear your heart on your sleeves. It was the longest interview I've ever had. A few hours later, with my fears out in the open, I was offered a chance to work a day at Insite to see if I would fit in there, and if I was ethically okay with the job I would have to do.

First day at Insite. I was greeted by the gummer, and it seemed like I was accepted. The regulars all had their own ways of testing me, and sure enough, I fit right in. I found that as I spent time with participants, I didn't struggle to see them as people. I grew up poor. I could have been any one of them, and it was only by the grace of God and the kindness of others that I walked a different path. It's not that hard to find yourself homeless. So, these were my brothers and sisters. But showing love doesn't mean enabling people. I wanted to make sure that I was joining Christ's redeeming work in the world, not petting the poor to make myself feel better. I was glad to be spending time with an unreached people group. Supervised consumption sites target injection drug users who spend their lives desperately seeking the next high. Some participants would come in as many as twenty times a day, spending their time between shooting up and turning tricks to get more dope. Insite was the only connection that this specific group had with the rest of the world. And I wanted to be there, to be part of their lives. The problem was that I couldn't bring myself to enable them to use illegal drugs.

My first big step out of my comfort zone was when I saw a guy come in who'd been in a couple of times already that day. It had been over three hours since the last time he was in, and he was shaking with withdrawal. He burst in, agitated and swearing, grabbed a couple of sterile needles and a spoon, and headed to a booth. He couldn't get the sterile water container open, so he spat

INTRODUCTION

in the spoon instead. I walked over and traded him the spit-filled spoon for a sterile one. He barely glanced up, and mixed his drugs in the sterile one fast. He looked at his arms, shot with injection marks and collapsed veins, and said, "Screw it." Instead he brought the syringe to his neck, hand shaking, desperate to end his withdrawals. I watched in shock as he just started stabbing wildly into his neck, missing his carotid artery by millimeters. Finally I found my voice. "Stop!" I yelled. "Let me find you a vein in your arm!" He ignored me and kept stabbing. Finally, he found his jugular vein, the one he was aiming for. I breathed a sigh of relief. I wasn't going to watch him bleed out in front of me. Not that day, anyway. After injecting, he glared at me. "You're new here. You don't got the right to tell me what to do with myself." It was my first lesson. Insite works as a community, not a dictatorship. I wasn't taken seriously just because I was a nurse. I had to prove that I actually cared before people would let me help. And that would take time.

I sat back down, a little crushed that the RN behind my name didn't automatically gain me respect. And then I realized—I had stepped outside my boundaries without even noticing. I panicked. Was it unchristian for me to offer to find that guy a vein? I was conflicted. In the moment, I knew that what I needed to do was try to save that man's life. But the more I thought about it, the more I second-guessed that gut reaction. Being present as he injected forced me into action, but in the freedom outside the reality of the moment, it was easier to forget that I was trying to save his life. Eventually I came to realize that the actual finding of the veins, or handing out of the needles, is only part of what Insite does. It's the side effect of spending time with people who use drugs.

See, if I was going to hang out with them and build relationships, I was going to have to meet them where they were. This necessitated being present as they injected, so if they overdosed they didn't die alone on the streets—I could bring them back. If we trusted each other, I could help prevent illness or injury—by bleeding out, getting a horrendous infection, or getting shot in the streets as they went out high and vulnerable. I couldn't help them if they were dead. Supervised consumption sites provide

INTRODUCTION

a safe place for people who use drugs to be out of their minds, without having to watch their backs for fear of being raped while under the influence. The core of what supervising consumption does, though, is simply being present with people as they inject themselves with drugs, regardless of whether or not the drugs are good for them. It means staying with them, helping to heal them, and bringing them back if they overdose. It's presence in the midst of the hardest times. This allows staff to build relationships with people who don't have another place to communicate with society. This literally was the byproduct of just showing up and being a part of the lives of this group of people. I realized that if I wanted to spend my time with people who use drugs, I wasn't going to be able to ignore the fact that some were shooting up using urine puddles as a source of liquid to inject, or were sharing needles in a community with a Hepatitis C rate of 90 percent. It wasn't a choice between helping them inject or having them not inject. It was a choice between helping them inject or watching as they died. If I was going to actively love this group of people, I was going to have to go all in. And so I started working at Insite.

These experiences formed the basis of my early days in addiction medicine. I would go on to write an article that became a topic of discussion in the Christian community. I did talks at various campuses and churches across the country, and I continued my work among shelter populations after moving back to Calgary. Much of this came to a halt when I started medical school in Calgary. Several years later, I graduated with a fellowship in addiction medicine—a trajectory that began on that fateful day at Insite. I now have the highest level of education in clinical addiction medicine that is currently available to Canadian doctors. I work in shelters, community clinics, and hospitals, performing addiction medicine as a physician with a variety of people. The opioid epidemic has hit, and together with COVID-19 it has created a dual disaster for people who struggle with addiction—whether homeless or wealthy. I have worked long hours trying to help in this dual epidemic, and have realized that much of what I do treats the patients in front of me, but it does not treat the circumstances they

INTRODUCTION

find themselves in. To do that, there needs to be a greater societal shift in understanding addiction medicine.

For me, this societal shift reflects the need for the church to do a better job following God. It means remembering that each of us, regardless of how we act or what we believe, are made in the image of God, are sacred, and have an incredible worth. It means that we must love sacrificially to help one another, to choose to be present with one another and not ostracize each other. God, in his infinite wisdom, came to us as a human, to be with us, to understand our struggles, and to sacrifice himself for us. This sacrificial, all-encompassing love is the critical feature of Christianity. It's also the one most easily lost in the noise of our world. I am so passionate about addiction medicine because I think it is the clearest way for me to practice what it means to love completely and extend the Grace I have received.

I don't quite know how to shift society, but I do know how my own views have shifted over time. To that end, each chapter in this book will use stories to "show my work" in coming to a moral and scientific understanding of a different aspect of addiction medicine. I'll go over some basic medical addiction-related concepts to start and explain the current state of affairs when it comes to the opioid crisis. I touch on the justice system and options for treatment for patients, and then I also speak to the complicity of the medical system. I will go over ways Christians have struggled to support my patients, and end by discussing what each of us can personally do to help make things better. I will tell stories of my patients, with alias names at times (denoted with an *) to protect their privacy.

It is my hope that this book also reflects my own personal journey toward God in serving this population. As I tell the stories that have shaped me, I hope that you will see the Divine in them, and that he will bring you to a richer understanding of how he is at work among people who are addicted.

The primary audience of this book is other Christians, because we work off of the same moral framework. The purpose of this book is to convince people who are already Christian that the

INTRODUCTION

practice of addiction medicine is also a practice of following Jesus. However, all are invited to read it, regardless of religious belief. This book is meant to be a reflection of my journey as a Christian addiction doctor—to read it, you do not have to be a Christian, and its goal is not to force you to become one. If mentions of Christianity trigger you to relive past trauma (recognizing that the church has also been complicit in the work of Satan through systemic and personal ways such as residential schools and many other evils), then this is probably not a book that will be helpful for you and you have my blessing to put it down and do something more fun like watch a full season of *Planet Earth*.

What I do hope for, for those of you who finish the book, is that you will see that I believe morality (and in my case religion) is actually very important in the discussion around addiction medicine, and for me, they are fully intertwined. I believe that God is the source of goodness, love, and justice in the world. Following him is my why—it's why I do what I do when the work is hard. I believe that developing the practice of looking for God in the staff and patients around me has taught me to see the divine at work in unexpected ways. And I hope that by reading this, you will too.

1

Addiction

It was a few minutes before we closed the clinic for the evening. A young woman walked in, well-dressed, nice bag, furtive eyes. She asked to speak to one of the doctors.

"Are you new here? You'll have to do an intake. Can you come back tomorrow?"

"No, please, I just want to talk to someone today."

The medical office assistant came to the back: "Anyone able to fit in this young lady?"

I came out to the waiting room to get her. She was standing nervously in front of the rows of empty plastic chairs and dusty silk trees in plastic pots. Her anxious expression looked out of place against the excessively cheery yellow walls of the waiting room.

She entered the clinic room, looking well put together but like she was about to fall apart. Her hair was up in a bun, and her lipstick was perfect—she had obviously fixed it before coming in because my lipstick never looks like that at the end of the day. She was trying her best.

"Hi Christine*, I'm Dr. Meera." I started my spiel. Welcome to the clinic. Standard confidentiality applies. Here's how we work. She nodded.

"Can you tell me what substances you use?"

Why I Help People Take Drugs

She cringed.

A few years ago, somebody T-boned me in my car. He ran the red, and nothing happened to him. Me on the other hand.... I was prescribed Percocets and T3s for the pain. They kept telling me it was short term, but they also kept refilling it. It stopped working so they switched me to oxycodone. I got a family doctor a few months ago, who told me I needed to stop. The problem is, it hurt so much. He tried to taper my pills. I got desperate, so I started snorting the pills because it helped the pain better.

About a month ago, I told my doctor—it took a lot for me, I was pretty ashamed. My doctor cut me off. He said it was for my own good. I tried really hard—I wanted to do what he said. But the withdrawals—I couldn't help myself. They made the pain three times worse. And I knew I needed the meds—I couldn't live without them. I couldn't stop thinking about them. I went to a walk-in; they said no. But there was this guy outside who said he knew what I was going through, and he had something that could help. He told me it was really potent, that I had to use small amounts or I'd overdose. He offered to sit with me while I tried it. I was so desperate. So I tried a little. He was right. It took the pain away. And it was cheap—so much cheaper than my prescriptions.

I started taking it more and more often. It just felt so good. You see, I'm engaged, but my boyfriend doesn't know I've been messing up. It's fine though. I don't take that much before work. I'm a nursing aide, so I can't be high while at work. So I just take enough to not have withdrawals. The high is between work and home—that's when I can really be myself without him watching. Since we met, he's always been watching. I can't see my friends, I can't even hang out with my family. But when I take the drugs, I feel safe like nothing that happens at home matters. At least for that one part of my day, nobody can hurt me. I can't even go back to the prescription strength stuff anymore, that's nothing compared to this.

ADDICTION

Christine's whole life just came pouring out to me, this stranger. She paused, and I handed her a tissue for her tears.

"But... I think I'm addicted now. Do you think it's an addiction?"

Gently, I nodded. "We have a standardized way to determine if someone has an addiction. It helps us come up with a diagnosis of a substance use disorder and determine the severity."

I was talking about the DSM-5 criteria for substance use disorder. It guides healthcare providers on the difference between substance use and a substance use disorder (or the difference between recreational use and addiction). It's easiest to wrap your mind around it by understanding how many of the psychiatric illnesses are diagnosed. I might have a lot of anxiety in general—some would call me an anxious person. This is simply part of how I am—I'm allowed to be an anxious person. But it's when this anxiety starts impacting my life negatively in tangible ways that harm me, that it becomes disordered. When this lasts too long, the diagnosis of Generalized Anxiety Disorder is given. Many of these diagnoses are based on how a person functions. It's fine to be an anxious person, but not if it means you can't go to work in the morning or have meaningful relationships because of debilitating anxiety. That's when you need to start thinking about treatment. It doesn't mean you can't work on your anxiety before it gets to this state. It just means it isn't a disorder.

Addiction works much the same way. Some people use drugs and don't get addicted. They don't have cravings, they don't have withdrawals, it doesn't impact their chosen lifestyle, and they have control and choice. This is not addiction. Addiction happens when people lose some measure of their God-given autonomy. They don't have as strong an ability to choose because the substance, or the behavior, has hijacked a primitive part of the brain that controls the urge to meet survival needs. Trying to stop is like telling your brain you don't need water when you're in the middle of the desert in +45 degree Celsius heat. There is a part of the brain that is designed to override your free will, to keep you alive. This is the part that substances can hijack. That's when addiction happens. This is why addiction is a medical issue by definition. You see, many people with addiction actually want to stop. They try their hardest. When they are told they need to have more faith, or pray harder, or have stronger willpower, it can be very demoralizing without this understanding of why it's not working. God embedded the survival instinct deep into people's brains to help them live. It's this instinct, albeit warped, that fuels addiction. It has gotten corrupted by the substance, but it's still as strong as our natural will to live. Willing against this instinct that God gave us is a complicated thing to do without a full understanding.

The goal of treating addiction is to help the brain develop new patterns—to break free from the urge to use and to realize that the substance or behavior is not required for survival. This takes a lot of mental energy, but it's a little bit like swimming perpendicular to the current. Please bear with me, I was a lifeguard many years before becoming a doctor, but I still have a water safety lecture in me just bubbling up and ready to come out.

If you get caught in a rip current, and you just try to swim back to shore, you'll get exhausted. The addiction is the current—it removes your choice and hijacks your brain so that even though you want to get back to shore, you're stuck. You can try to muscle through and stop the substances and swim directly against the current back to shore. This is like "just try to stop using." It might work, but most of the time it doesn't. Factors that impact this might be how strong the current is, how long you've been stuck in it, how far from shore you are, and how good a swimmer you were to begin with. These are all things that are no longer modifiable once you're out in the ocean, stuck in a current. But if you can swim sideways out of the current, you might have a chance. You'll still be out in deep water, exhausted, and with a long way to go. But you're out of the current. This is how we treat addiction. We try to get people out of the current, so they regain some freedom and choice. Then, we try to support them on their long swim back to shore. Some people make it. Some don't.

For the young lady in my office, she was well caught into the current. There are eleven different criteria[1] that we use to assess if

---

1. American Psychiatric Association, "Substance-related and Addictive Disorders," 541.

ADDICTION

somebody has a substance use disorder or not. You need at least two of these criteria over ideally a twelve-month period to diagnose addiction.

1. Often taken in larger amounts or for a longer period than was intended.
2. A persistent desire or unsuccessful efforts to cut down or control use.
3. A great deal of time is spent in activities necessary to obtain, use, or recover from the substance's effects.
4. Craving or a strong desire or urge to use the substance.
5. Recurrent use resulting in a failure to fulfill major role obligations at work, school, or home.
6. Continued use despite having persistent or recurrent social or interpersonal problems caused or exacerbated by its effects.
7. Important social, occupational, or recreational activities are given up or reduced because of use.
8. Recurrent use in situations in which it is physically hazardous.
9. Continued use despite knowledge of having a persistent or recurrent physical or psychological problem that is likely to have been caused or exacerbated by the substance.
10. Tolerance: Needing more of the substance to have the same effect.*
11. Withdrawals: When you stop, you get symptoms that go away if you start again.*

Mild: 2–3 criteria. Moderate: 4–5 criteria. Severe: 6 or more criteria.
*These two don't apply for prescribed medications when taken as directed.

Christine fit into a "severe" categorization of substance use disorder. She was just at the point of recognizing addiction in herself, and she was already deep into the current. (As a side note, if you have read this and identified that you may fall into the category of having a substance use disorder, it's best not to self-diagnose. I don't even treat my family members, because it's too close to be able to be objective. I recommend talking to a family doctor about your concerns.)

Early diagnosis could have made Christine's journey a lot easier. There were lots of places along the way that would have made her journey better, and we'll get into some of them later in the book. Her family doctor saw her behavior as frustrating and willful, instead of recognizing addiction. The doctors that filled her prescriptions along the way didn't ask the screening questions that would have identified addiction earlier. Her chronic pain wasn't treated with psychotherapy and a wrap-around program (more on this to come in further chapters). She didn't get counseling after her accident, which would have helped her realize that having an injustice happen like her car crash actually puts her at higher risk of chronic pain issues if she can't accept it and move into a new reality for herself. Acceptance and commitment therapy could have been really helpful for her, but it wasn't offered.

There are other risk factors that impact how well Christine does "in the current." Her description of her boyfriend raises red flags for domestic abuse. Her profession leads to increased stigma around substance use, and she would risk losing her job if she disclosed. She is physically dependent on the opioids. She is ashamed of herself and isolated.

She also is at risk of death. We are currently in the middle of an opioid crisis that is getting worse every day. People are dying at unprecedented rates. Every time she uses, she plays a deadly roulette.

I held her hand, and I explained addiction to her. Addiction is a chronic illness. It follows the same pattern as many other chronic illnesses like diabetes or hypertension. It is unlikely to ever be cured. You could be 99 years old with half a century of sobriety under your belt, and when your partner dies, you'll still be at risk to think about using. But even if the triggers remain, addiction can be managed. The harms of addiction can be reduced. If caught early, like diabetes, sometimes lifestyle modification and psychotherapy is enough to stall it in its tracks. If caught later, (like diabetes), sometimes you need medication (like insulin) in order to reduce the harm that the illness does to your body. Either way, this thing can be brought under control. It is possible to treat addiction and to regain a normal life. This is not possible for everyone, just like some people will die of diabetes. But some people will also live full and healthy lives with it. We need to do our best and use everything in our arsenal to treat it, to give people that chance. Addiction medicine has come a long way, and the arsenal with which we fight is constantly growing. The practice of addiction medicine is one of choosing hope.

And hope can be hard to find when we talk about the potency of the drugs on the streets nowadays. The more common drugs can be classed primarily into alcohol, opioids, stimulants, and benzodiazepines. All of these drugs affect dopamine, one of the body's natural neurochemicals that regulate pleasure. Sex, good food, and laughter with friends have all been shown to increase the brain's levels of dopamine. The body develops a range of natural dopamine, and creates a baseline level. This means that most days the levels of pleasure are normal, and then sometimes when something really good happens, the dopamine spikes. Medications to treat depression also try to improve dopamine levels. The problem with drugs and alcohol is they can raise dopamine levels unnaturally high. This means that a hug no longer feels like anything, in comparison to the drug itself. The body copes by increasing the number of receptors, meaning that the proportion of receptors filled by a hug is now not even enough to get to a baseline state of happiness. More and more drugs are needed to fill the receptors just to get to a baseline, and highs become unattainable anymore. People are stuck using drugs just to get by.

The increased potency of street drugs has led to an increased need for higher and higher doses of drugs. Opioids are fueling the death rates currently. Street opioids used to be the potency of heroin or oxycodone. Now, they are several orders of magnitude more potent. One point of fentanyl, basically the smallest unit of measuring street fentanyl, is theoretically 0.1 grams of fentanyl. In the hospital, we typically treat patients with micrograms of fentanyl.

Why I Help People Take Drugs

Doing the math, 1 point of fentanyl is theoretically equivalent to 10,000 milligrams of morphine. (A typical dose for someone who is not used to opioids and has acute pain in the emergency department might be 5–10 milligrams of morphine). Some patients will consume 30 points of fentanyl in a day. The potency is unprecedented. Carfentanil is still more concentrated. The potency makes seeking a high more attainable, but it also comes with a high risk of death due to opioid toxicity, which causes the body to stop breathing. Several people live on the line between trying to feel some pleasure, and dying. It's not an enviable position.

Sometimes, people prefer to use methamphetamines rather than opioids. Meth is a stimulant drug, and it has similar synthetic derivatives. It too increases dopamine levels, often higher than any other drug. It may not cause people to stop breathing, but for some it does cause their brains to dissociate and go into a state of psychosis. They may have a complete psychotic break when intoxicated, and may run into traffic or pick at their skin for fear of bugs. Sometimes people who use meth become violent. They are unable to assess reality. This doesn't happen to all people who use meth, but it happens often enough to be a known side effect. Meth-induced psychosis is associated with a higher rate of developing schizophrenia in the long term. Other less potent stimulants include cocaine or crack cocaine. It's hard to find cocaine that isn't actually mixed with meth in my city now, because meth is cheaper and more potent, and a little bit livens up a batch of cocaine.

Benzodiazepines are a form of "down," like opioids. They cause respiratory depression as well, and it often lasts longer than the opioids do. To make the fentanyl more potent, so people can feel it more, dealers have been adding benzos to the mix. This vastly increases the risk of overdose, and worse, it reduces the person's ability to come back. You see the antidote for opioids is naloxone, or Narcan. People carry naloxone kits around, ready to administer them to someone who is overdosing. I have one in my purse, and one in my car. They are free at pharmacies and are just as important as knowing CPR. But naloxone does not reverse benzodiazepines, only opioids. This means that naloxone alone is sometimes ineffective at reversing an overdose.

Alcohol, a legal over-the-counter drug on the list, is not off the hook. More people die due to alcohol-related factors than almost any other reason. And with an increasingly isolating society, alcohol use disorder is on the rise. Alcohol, when mixed with opioids or benzodiazepines, or when taken in high doses, also causes people to stop breathing and die. Alcohol plays a significant part in the opioid crisis because it increases the risk of death by overdose. As if it didn't have enough toxicities just on its own.

We haven't talked much about cannabis or tobacco, natural plants that when smoked can cause significant harm in the long run. Lung cancer and emphysema due to tobacco use disorder are also deadly consequences—these are other ways that addiction can cause harm.

I don't address other hallucinogens much because most are primarily used recreationally and not addictively. They are less addictive and it is rare that a primary substance of use is a hallucinogen like MDMA. Harms can still come from them, but it's unusual to find someone fully addicted to them. And of course there are also behavioral addictions, like internet addictions, video games, gambling, and sex. These are classified differently, and have a different potency depending on the age of the brain that is affected. They are largely outside the scope of this book so I will only mention them here. Still, they follow similar mechanisms to the substance use disorders, and still often require medical interventions.

Addiction, by definition, involves a loss of freedom—a slavery to the substance. I believe in a God who breaks the chains of slavery and wants freedom for us all. This is why I practice addiction medicine—I wanted to join in this work that God is doing in the world. It may look different for each patient, and it's not always successful, but each step toward freedom is a blessing to witness.

One morning back when I was a shelter nurse, staff asked me to take a look at a patient. He had been dropped off in the middle of the night by police, and they were worried that he did not look well. I walked through the building, people lying on the floor around me. It looked like a warehouse dotted with blankets and blue gym mats. The smell of old socks and stale beer hit me as soon as I stepped in the room. Checking the mat plan, I found the patient they were worried about. He was unresponsive, with salt and pepper hair, bare arms despite the cold, and his arms stiffly curled under his chin. Non-medical shelter staff had called paramedics (EMS) in the middle of the night, but EMS reported that the patient had been transported by police from the hospital to the shelter, and he did not require further assessment.

One look at the patient, and I knew. He had a brain injury. His arms were posturing in a classic "neurologic damage" kind of way. When I pulled open his eyelids, his pupils were unequal and unreactive. My pulse quickened and sweat filled my forehead—I knew this was bad. I called EMS, and told them to get there fast. They came, and they took him to the hospital.

It turns out, the patient had presented to the hospital, belligerent, shouting, and cursing. He threw a chair in the hospital lobby, and was escorted out by security before seeing a doctor or a nurse. The police were called. He was deemed to have been intoxicated, and passed out in the back of the police car. Police carried him into the shelter, and laid him on a mat. Staff waited for him to wake up to check him in because nobody recognized him. Morning came, and he was still not awake.

When EMS answered my call, they found his wallet. It turned out he had never been to the shelter before. He was not homeless, and he had no substances in his system. What he had was a stroke, a bleed in his brain, that had caused him to act in an agitated and delirious way. This was not recognized or diagnosed until it was too late. The patient died in the hospital.

He did not have an addiction, as far as we know. He died because he was presumed to have been intoxicated. This story, while not uncommon, was the first time I was faced with such an injustice. Because it's not just about what addiction is. It's about knowing the stigma addiction carries is so strong that people are

ADDICTION

rightfully afraid of being painted with the same brush. This man died because someone assumed he had an addiction. The fear of being considered to have an addiction is strong, and it spurs things like mockery or cruelty. Many people who struggle with homelessness are not addicted and do not use substances. They too are deserving of dignity and care. They just aren't the people that this book is about. It is important to acknowledge that the stigma of addiction causes damage not just to people who have addictions, but also to people who don't.

One of my patients was a tall, big, Indigenous man named Peter*. When I say tall, I mean when you stood beside him, you felt like a toddler. He would have been scary if he wasn't so sweet. He was known everywhere as the guy who would share whatever he had. His kindness led to him being taken advantage of over and over again. He kept losing his housing because he would bring over friends who were still homeless—they would party and be destructive, and he would get evicted. He suffered from schizophrenia, as well as a very traumatic childhood. His desire to be connected and to be included, combined with his inability to set boundaries, got him into trouble regularly. One time, he was beaten badly by someone he thought was a friend, and was left to die. Peter spent a month in the ICU before making a miraculous recovery.

Although his ways were often inadvisable, and I spent many hours trying to convince him that boundaries matter, Peter somehow kept finding himself in difficult situations. He drank to cope, and he drank to be social. He worked closely with the housing program for one of the shelters he stayed at, and he kept getting evicted for guest behaviors. Still, he worked hard on trying to develop boundaries, and together with the program he decided he was able to be housed again. He got a viewing for a place in the neighborhood where his church was. Peter was part of a neighborhood church, full of people who were much older than him, but he loved them and they loved him. He was so excited to live near the church. He felt that he was set up for success with this housing placement, because he could finally integrate into a healthy community.

So a week before his housing viewing, Peter tried to get into detox. Alcohol withdrawal can be fatal, and he had previously had severe withdrawal where he had seizures. Stopping cold turkey can be dangerous—he needed medical supervision at a detox facility. Neither of the city's two detox centers could take him. He lined up at 6 a.m., two days in a row. Still nothing. So he stubbornly decided he was going to stop drinking anyway. I was called into the shelter, where I saw him convulsing on a mat. He was having a seizure. I called EMS. His seizure stopped, but he was very confused. Two paramedics arrived, and asked him if he wanted to "come with us." They leaned over him in their uniforms, and despite his size, he was afraid. He said no. They left. He seized again. I called EMS, again. The paramedics took much longer to arrive. He seized for over ten minutes. I timed it as we waited for EMS, helpless, kneeling on the floor of the shelter over the blue mats, without medication or IV supplies, trying to put a pillow under his head to keep him safe. They came, injected him with medication, and loaded him into the ambulance. I finished up some paperwork in the shelter, then left for the hospital.

In the emergency room, I found Peter behind some curtains on a stretcher. He was conscious, but looked rough. He was hooked up to a cardiac monitor, which surprised me. I checked his chart and learned that he'd had a heart attack while in the ambulance. The paramedics had been able to revive him, and now here he was lying in front of me, with a sheepish grin. "I'm gonna get housed if it kills me," he said, trying not to crack up at his own joke. I glared at him. I was about to start lecturing him, when the emergency room doctor came by the stretcher. I introduced myself and asked which unit he was likely to be admitted to. The ER doc looked at me. "This guy's a drunk Native. He's gonna die a drunk Native. Nothing I do is going to fix that. He isn't going to take up a bed here; I'm not admitting him." And the doc walked away. I was stunned. Rage built up inside me that I didn't know how to let out, so I did the most impotent and useless thing I could—I started crying. Peter, who heard the whole thing, grabbed my hand. He looked me in the eye and said: "Hey, relax. Remember. God loves him too."

This was the reaction of one of society's most vulnerable people, who had gotten used to being hurt. He somehow still had the strength to choose a path of grace. I saw it as a lack of boundaries, and I was so frustrated with him giving repeated chances to "friends" who were taking advantage of him. He looked at them, saw that they were taking advantage of him, and chose still to see them with love, the way God did. Peter had practiced how to love in the face of hurt.

Addiction has many faces, and some of the stories I will share in this book will hopefully help reveal some more about how it affects people. It is my hope that this will broaden your perspective on what addiction can look like, and help keep your eyes open to how God is working in the lives of people with addictions.

2

Crisis

ADDICTION IS SOMETHING THAT has been written about for ages. It is not a new illness or a new concept. Paul himself wrote words that echo through the hearts of many people living with addiction:

> I do not understand what I do. For what I want to do I do not do, but what I hate I do. . . . For I have the desire to do what is good, but I cannot carry it out. For I do not do the good I want to do, but the evil I do not want to do—this I keep on doing. Now if I do what I do not want to do, it is no longer I who do it, but it is sin living in me that does it. (Romans 7:15, 18b–20, NIV)

While Paul's letter to the Romans was written for a specific people in a specific time and place, there are truths in it that apply to us all today. I see addiction through this lens—it is an affliction that is shared among all of humanity. We find ways to categorize it in terms of legalities or severities, but the reality is, we all struggle with the basic concept of doing things we do not want to do. There is nothing new under the sun. Even Paul could not harness the willpower to stop certain behaviors. Even Paul could not pray enough to end his sin. This is a human affliction, and Paul's vulnerability in sharing his struggles helps us all to understand our own need for God.

I feel Paul's words inside me every single day as I am made aware of the multitude of ways I live outside of my values. In little ways and in big ways, we all sin against ourselves, against one another, and against the land we are given to care for. This is the relief of grace—that our sin is known, that we are loved despite it, and that we are invited into that love just as we are. To know this level of grace, and then to turn to one another in judgment, is also something we humans tend to do. This is why in the Lord's Prayer we are guided to ask God to help us forgive others as he forgives us. We need constant reminders that we have received grace and must therefore extend it outward.

Although the struggle with doing things that we do not want to do affects all of us, for those struggling with opioid addiction it has taken a turn recently toward greater darkness. We now live in a time where imminent death is often an unfortunate consequence of substance use. This is not because of the addiction itself, because addiction has been around for ages. It is because of the environment we currently live in. We live in a world where certain types of addiction are required to remain hidden, and where we turn a blind eye to the harms they cause.

People who use drugs are at higher risk of death by opioid toxicity today than they used to be because of the amount of fentanyl and other toxic substances in the supply that have popped up in the last few years. I have been practicing in addiction medicine since before the current opioid epidemic, and I can say that there has been a marked change in severity of harms of addiction in the past few years. People used to die of overdose, but not nearly at the rates they are dying now.

Every day when I check my documents inbox, I've learned to brace my heart to expect medical examiners' requests for information. I've had to grieve that another patient whose story I was privy to, whose life I had been a part of, is gone. Each time this happens, I pick up the phone, calling caseworkers and nurses, breaking the bad news. "Are you okay?" I ask. "Call if you need to talk." We take care of each other in this field, because we have to.

A medical student who watched this process with horror one morning recently asked me how I cope with the death and what I do to protect my heart. I wish that I could "not care" about each death. The problem is, once you know somebody and they've shared this difficult deep part of themselves with you, it's impossible not to root for them. You love them for who they are because they're human, they're in your path, and they are inherently deserving of love. You hope and pray that they'll live, so that one day they can thrive. But in the current state of affairs, people are neither thriving nor living.

As I write this, several people die in my province of Alberta each day from opioid toxicity. Between January 2020 and July 2021, there were approximately 3,000 opioid deaths in BC, compared to the approximately 1,800 people who died from COVID-19. To be sure, the reason that the deaths from COVID were so limited was due to the robust public health interventions that were put into place. Those interventions are lacking when it comes to opioid use disorder.

The opioid epidemic came first, long before COVID became part of our vernacular. Patients were dropping like flies, tricked by the toxicity of the drug supply that they were completely dependent on. We scrambled, trying to put into place naloxone kit programs and supervised consumption sites, trying desperately to keep people alive so they'd have a chance to recover. It helped a little, but each intervention was still a drop in the ocean. Fentanyl had changed the game.

The current opioid epidemic, combined with the COVID pandemic, which is ongoing as I write this, sometimes means that I forget what life was like before either. In the crisis of the moment, I am called to react and to provide the best care that I can. But these practices are constantly changing depending on the environment I find myself in. Addiction medicine is a rapidly changing field, and often guidelines that are two or three years old are woefully outdated. Many of the medications I use to treat addiction today were not yet available when I was a medical resident. Addiction medicine needs to change as fast as the drug supply changes. This means that we are constantly reassessing what is safe and what is not.

My home province is not alone in battling an opioid crisis. Because of geography, much of Canada and the US are all seeing serious problems with fentanyl use. In the US, 92,000 people died of drug-related overdose in 2020 alone. New York responded by opening up supervised consumption sites, and other states across the country are looking into the same thing. These are helpful measures, but they feel like too little too late for the families of those who have died. My own propensity is to see these statistics as large numbers, instead of considering the families that have been impacted. I just don't have the emotional capacity to hold the weight of all that pain. But God does. I know that God is present with those families as they grieve. He knew every hair on the head of each person who died. He knew their stories, knew the pain that caused them to use fentanyl. He was with them in the end.

Incredibly potent, fentanyl often kills. Before it does, though, it gives you the best high of your life. The high has been described by patients as "I felt loved for the first time," or, "I could finally imagine what life without rape could have been like," or, "It was like the joy of seeing my sister again." A little bit of fentanyl goes a long way toward healing a hurt heart. But like any quick fix or miracle treatment for trauma, it comes at a cost. Fentanyl causes severe respiratory depression that makes people stop breathing. This lack of oxygenation can cause brain damage, muscle damage, and death. For someone with an opioid use disorder, their brain has suffered a loss of control despite these consequences. Many know the risks and keep using. Many others wonder why. The answer lies in brain chemistry. People lose control. They use despite negative consequences. They use compulsively, answering to cravings. These actions are processed in the limbic system of the brain, the part that processes functions required for life, not the part that makes conscious choices. The limbic brain has been tricked into thinking the drug is required for life. It will do anything to trick the conscious part of the mind into acquiring more. Individual decision-making is not the focus of the picture anymore.

Interestingly, these concepts are accepted as part of humanity in general. With COVID, although certainly there was an emphasis placed on each individual's responsibility to care for one another, wear masks, wash hands, etc., there were still systemic public health interventions put into place. There is a recognition in public health that with any spate of deaths, interventions need to be tailored at both an individual and a population level in order to make change.

For the past couple of years I worked seven days a week, on call more nights than not, trying to help the homeless sector who was hit especially hard by COVID. I helped create addiction medicine protocols that were implemented to care for those at Calgary's first assisted self-isolation space, which was brought to life to provide patients who are homeless with somewhere to stay. I broke the news to patients in shelters that they were COVID-positive and held them as they cried. My comfort felt inadequate when trying to hug patients wrapped in a yellow gown and goggles, wearing a surgical cap that my friend sewed for me as her way to help protect me. I treated patients with addiction who were COVID-positive in the hospital, trying to figure out if the shaking was from fever or from withdrawal. On the few off hours I had, I wrestled with figuring out the difference between a will and a personal directive (you should have both). I listened as patients asked if they were going to die, and I wondered the same for myself. Working in the hospital and in shelters, directly with patients who had COVID, the exhaustion was very real. Christmas of 2020 was spent working at the self-isolation site with my friends. I celebrated the birth of Jesus by trying my best to love and to heal. People were dying all around me—far more from opioids than from COVID. Isolated and scared to access shelter, people were using alone and unsafely. The opioid deaths spiked.

Prior to and continuing through the pandemic, the Alberta government announced the closure of supervised consumption sites and medical clinics designed to treat severe opioid use disorder. It scaled back life-saving interventions, following public sentiment around funding treatment for opioid use. This wasn't strictly the fault of the government—they were responding to the will of the people. The public strongly voiced a lack of trust in science, and placed their faith in faulty preconceived notions about addiction. This voice has echoed all across North America.

As a Christian, my most important and highest calling is to seek God out in his work in the world, and join in. It is tricky to figure out where he is sometimes, but I find that it's easiest if I am present. Presence in a homeless shelter, day after day, week after week, makes it easier to see how exactly love flows through those places. Presence in a hospital privileges me with seeing God in the worry of family members desperately trying to care for their loved ones. And science is the attempt to be as present as possible in the less obvious workings of the world. I believe that God made this world with order and structure, and learning about it helps us to better follow God's will.

Science allows for a nonjudgmental space to learn about things like how the body works, where we bring in our questions and our guesses but allow these hypotheses to be confirmed or rejected. It is a humbling recognition that humanity is not all-powerful and does not know everything. I personally approach science as a way to do my best to know how to heal. This is, for me, what it means to be a Christian doctor. I study the science, and I use that knowledge to help the best way I can, knowing that it will be imperfect, but trusting that God is present. Facts based in science are simply a description of the world that God loves, and to deny them is to risk denying what God has put in place. Sure, people can present falsehoods as facts, but when reported through scientific means, this is far less likely. The best defense against fake news is the rigor and integrity of the scientific method—or as I would call it, the best way to objectively study the world God has made. Science tells us, through statistics and toxicology reports, that God has now witnessed the death of thousands of people that he loves, because of our inability to treat opioid use disorder.

COVID has worsened the opioid epidemic significantly. Not having regular access to trafficked opium and heroin has led to the further dependence on synthetic drugs made in Canada, like fentanyl and carfentanil. Fear of catching COVID leads people to use alone, to avoid shelters, and to use quickly—a recipe for death.

Not having others nearby means there is nobody to intervene quickly in case of an overdose. Avoiding shelters exposes people to the elements, causing increased risk of frostbite and isolating people away from sources of help. Using drugs quickly because they are in public and do not want to risk arrest causes people to take risks and not carefully measure out the amounts they can tolerate. This again increases risk of overdose. On top of that, the closure of supervised consumption sites, and the closure of some opioid clinics to new patients, has largely flown under the radar due to media focus on COVID. All of these measures worsen the situation for people who use drugs.

Patients are finding new and creative ways to cope with the dual pandemic. One such patient was isolated in his apartment a few months ago. He couldn't get money to use opioids, his drug of choice, and he was COVID-positive. He didn't want to pass it on to others.

I got a phone call from the staff at the harm-reduction building he was staying at. "I have a weird question for you."

Thinking privately in my arrogance that I was experienced and could easily answer, I said: "I'm sure it's not weird. Fire away."

"Okay, so Doug* on the second floor has been making alcohol in his bathtub. He tells us he wears a mask anytime he's in there, and he keeps everything sanitary. He's been leaving cups of it outside his door. Other residents of the building have been taking the alcohol and leaving him cash. Doug just tested positive for COVID. Does this mean they're all now close contacts?"

I racked my brain. So many factors were at play. Was the alcohol made in the same bathroom that Doug used? What was the actual alcohol content? Was Doug symptomatic or still infectious? Was the transfer done in a sterile way? And separate from the question around COVID transmission, was the alcohol safe to drink? Was Doug using the cash to buy opioids? What was the overdose risk? In addition to all these questions was the question of what we would do if the whole building was exposed to the patient? Where would they all go? Who would enforce isolation?

Fitting substance use disorders into a pandemic has forced the creativity of addiction medicine and public health to find ways to support these patients. I phoned my friend, a public health doctor, and we tried to figure out what to do and how to keep the most people safe. We worked together to try our best.

While I was trying to figure out a plan, I received another phone call. A colleague of mine's name showed up on the caller ID. We had done our family medicine residency together. I answered it.

"Hey Meera. I'm really sorry to tell you this, but I wanted you to know that one of your patients passed away in the hospital."

"Who was it?"

"Felicity Straten.*"

I sat stunned at the name. Felicity had been my patient for years, first when I worked as a nurse, then as a doctor. I knew her family, had met her kids. Felicity had been doing really well and had maintained sobriety for the past six months.

"What happened?" The cause of death was unclear. Yesterday, we received the toxicology report. "Fentanyl toxicity." I knew it.

Patients who have maintained sobriety for a while are at much higher risk of death by overdose. It happens just when they're doing well, they've been off drugs for a while, their tolerance has dropped, and their lives are starting to normalize. Relapse at that stage can be deadly. Felicity had been lost just when things had started coming together for her.

I went home and watched an episode of Ted Lasso. Season 1, episode 10. It was entitled, "The Hope that Kills You." It struck a chord. I tend to call myself a "realist" instead of an optimist, which really just stems from self-protection. I don't want to get my hopes up for fear of being disappointed. It's the hope that kills you. The practice of caring for and loving my patients is a practice of choosing hope against the odds. It is to love in the face of death, to choose to allow my heart to be broken, time and again, by witnessing death steal away the sacred faces I have come to cherish.

There will come a time when this opioid epidemic fades, when the supply becomes safe again, and when the death rates come back down. When that happens, addiction will still exist.

One day, a new threat may appear, a new drug that causes worrisome side effects. Addiction medicine practitioners will keep doing the best we can to heal, to keep people alive, and to reduce the harms of addiction. We will keep trying to treat people with addiction and bring them to health. We will not stop being creative in our solutions, doing our best to bring hope in an ever-changing world where the only constant is our shared humanity.

Tomorrow, I will go back to clinic. I will check my documents inbox, and prepare my heart for the lives that have been lost. I will pray, knowing that we have clear medical interventions that may have saved them, if our society had wanted to. I will grieve, both for the patient, and for the world that turned a blind eye to them. And I will continue to believe that people can change, that God can work miracles, and that society will one day grow to love these patients the way God does.

3

Trauma

IN PREPARATION FOR MY next patient, I read their recent discharge summary from the hospital. "Twenty-three-year-old female presented with cellulitis and abscess due to intravenous drug use. Received twenty-four hours of IV antibiotics in hospital then stepped down to oral antibiotics, per the infectious disease specialists to facilitate discharge. Discharge plan: Continue full course of oral antibiotics. Advised to stop using methamphetamines." This was a patient who was admitted to the hospital with an infection in their arm from missing a vein while injecting meth.

Mari* came into the room jerkily, carrying several plastic bags full of belongings, talking a mile a minute, picking at her face. "She looks like she's still using meth," I thought to myself. She sat down and I got her a paper cup full of water. It was hot outside.

"How's your arm doing? Can I see?" I took a look. Full of track marks and small red infections, her skin was excoriated and bruised. It wasn't swollen, though. The antibiotics were working and her infection was improving.

"What happened? How come you missed the vein that time?"

"I was rushing. I was so tired, and was set up in this doorway in an alley. I had run out of sterile water, but there was this pretty clean puddle. There were some guys that had been following me and I thought I lost them but I could hear them down the end of the alley, setting up their camp. I was trying to hide; I didn't want to come out to go get supplies. And I didn't want to fall asleep. I've been down that path before, you know, where you wake up to a nightmare."

I knew. I had first met Mari a year prior—an outreach van chased three guys off of her in an alley. She was naked from the waist down, semi-conscious with facial fractures, and crying. They took her to the hospital. A rape kit wasn't done right away because she had alcohol in her system—they needed to wait for her to be sober before they could get her consent to do it. As she sobered up, she couldn't cope with what had just happened, and she left the hospital to go numb the pain elsewhere. Outreach teams had tried to find her, to convince her to go back to the hospital. Mari wouldn't agree. She couldn't stand the way the nurses looked at her.

We had been working on trying to find her housing. The waitlist was several years long. She was too well, too high functioning. It was shelters or the streets for her, and shelters had predators like the guys who did this to her. Like a gazelle avoiding a watering hole because of fear of lions in the grass, Mari slept outside, hiding, trying to survive. Her mother had died a couple years prior of opioid toxicity (overdose). Her father lived in a rooming house with his buddies, drinking and using. He had lent her out a few times before to get money for more alcohol. She had no supports in town.

"How old were you when you first used alcohol?"
"Eight."
"What about the first time you injected any drugs?"
"Twelve."
"How old were you when you first had any sexual encounter?"
"Eight. My uncle."

The story made sense. Trauma, untreated, had shaped Mari's story until she was a twenty-three-year-old woman who had been injecting hard drugs for over a decade. My job, on paper, was to support her in her goal of stopping using meth. But she used the meth to stay awake so she wouldn't get raped again. She used it to numb the fears and erase the memories. And she used it because her brain never had a chance to develop healthy patterns and to learn how to channel her survival instincts in a socially helpful way. The frontal lobe in the brain that helps with executive function, decision-making, and risk-taking behaviors is not fully developed until about twenty-five years old. Drugs impair this part of the brain and prevent it from developing. Brain-wise, this was a girl, not a woman.

We talk about choosing to work with "vulnerable populations" to refer to patients who are marginalized by society. But I rarely stop to think about what makes a patient actually vulnerable. People who are marginalized are much more likely to suffer severe negative health outcomes. Those who experienced trauma in childhood? Even more so.

The CDC-Kaiser Permanente Adverse Childhood Experiences (ACE) Study is one of the largest investigations of childhood abuse and neglect and household challenges and later-life health and well-being. The original ACE Study was conducted at Kaiser Permanente from 1995 to 1997 with two waves of data collection. Over 17,000 Health Maintenance Organization members from Southern California receiving physical exams completed confidential surveys regarding their childhood experiences and current health status and behaviors.[1]

Adverse childhood experiences were directly correlated with a higher risk of things like depression or substance use. What was more surprising to me was that they were also directly correlated with things like cancer, diabetes, or heart attack, independent of substance use or lifestyle. Things that could not be explained by psychoanalysis. This suggests that trauma and adversity has a toxicity on the body that acts similar to carcinogens or other poisons. It physically harms the body later in life. This link between toxic stress in early childhood and poor health later in adulthood is well known and prevalent now because it was studied. But it's just the start of our exploration into the effects that trauma has on people. Studies looking into generational trauma, for example, are just beginning.

1. Felitti et al., "Relationship of Childhood Abuse," 245–58.

What's clear is the vast majority of my patients have trauma in their past. This can be severe, but it also can look like mild family dysfunction. It all contributes to this complex tapestry that impacts addiction. It also makes it hard to just "stop using drugs." Drugs alone are rarely ever the lone cause of addiction or addiction-related harms.

Trauma is treatable, and there are a variety of therapies to treat it. Unsurprisingly, nearly all of these therapies are not covered by standard health services in Alberta. Nonprofit organizations are forced to hire trauma therapists in order to care for their patients—this is not a readily accessible service. Often, trauma therapy requires a certain amount of stability in patients before commencing. But patients who are very vulnerable can't get that stability before their trauma is treated. This leads to a cycle where people who are vulnerable and traumatized are left to fend for themselves on the street.

Which brings us back to Mari. I had tried to get her into detox, but she was not ready yet. She couldn't envision being sober and having to cope with all the things that had happened to her. I had her on the wait-list to see a counselor, but it would be several months because she missed her intake appointment. All I could do was be present. Whenever she showed up, I'd try to spend some time with her—to build rapport and help her feel a little less alone. I would keep encouraging her to use sterile water and sterile supplies to inject, to learn to value herself and her body. I'd see a nail polish in the store in her favorite color, and hold onto it in my bag with the hopes that the next time I see her, I could give her the polish.

And of course, I prayed for Mari. On my own time, of course, and never in front of her. She didn't need that added complication in her life and we weren't in a place where that was a conversation that should be had. But it was important to me that I prayed. I prayed that she would be able to see how special she was, and learn to love herself the way I am sure God loves her. I prayed for her to see love, to see peace, and to have goodness and kindness play a larger role in her life. I prayed for her to get into counseling.

I prayed for her safety, that she would stay alive. I prayed to the Healer that she would be healed. Drugs just didn't seem like the main thing to be praying about. Because the point is that drugs were not the point.

More evidence is coming to light about trauma being passed down from generation to generation in the DNA of people who are traumatized. These changes reinforce what many have been trying to say—generational trauma is a real and impactful barrier to health. Populations that have struggled with generational trauma are over-represented in addiction medicine. Patients who are Indigenous, descendants of slaves, or newly landed with parents who grew up in refugee camps are all overrepresented due to not only their own traumas, but the traumas that came before them. The impact of residential schools reverberates to this day, with the last one in Canada being closed in 1996. So the treatment of addiction needs to include not only drug-specific treatments, but reconciliation on a larger level. As society starts to name the wrongs that have been done, and starts to work toward healing, this work will indirectly affect the work I do to treat addiction. The recognition of generational trauma is a big step for medicine, and as further research comes to light, treating the trauma will lead to healthier populations.

I was in the hospital, going through an intake with a new consult. Drew* was in his forties, wearing tight jeans and a rodeo belt buckle. The reason for consult stated "alcohol abuse."

He was sitting in bed, one jean leg pulled up. He had been admitted for an infected surgical site in his ankle. He had been in a cab a month ago, and it had gotten T-boned. The ankle surgery had gone well, but now there were complications. The nurse rolled her eyes when I walked past—"He won't get changed into a gown."

I sat down beside the bed. He smiled at me charmingly. "Thanks for trying to help me." We went through the questionnaire.

"How many drinks would you say you drink per day?"

"On a good day, probably twenty-six ounces. On a less good day, maybe half that."

Drew explained that he drank most days, trying to numb the pain, bored. I asked him about his income. "Royalties." It turns out he was a country singer, famous I suppose, although I hadn't heard of him. A later internet search revealed several popular music videos from when he'd made it big in Nashville.

We discussed anti-craving medication and the risk for withdrawal. He told me he would love a medication to help with the cravings. I asked him about his medication coverage. "NIHB," he said. He had First Nations status and some medications were covered under this. Fortunately, the one I wanted to start him on would be covered.

"Before I go, I want to talk about mental health concerns. Many patients who struggle with substance use disorders have a history of trauma. If this has happened to you, I want you to know that it can be treated. Medications and therapy can help ease the burden of trauma, and may help with treating the alcohol use disorder as well."

Drew's face darkened and his lips tightened. The silence in the room was palpable.

"You don't have to feel like this is something you need to talk about right now with me."

He relaxed a bit, exhaling. "Yeah, yeah I'd like to talk another time."

The next day, I stopped by his room again. We chatted about the unusual heat wave, and the colors of the larches in the morning. I'd started him on a medication to help with his alcohol cravings, and so far, so good—he didn't have side effects after the first dose. As I was heading out the door, he called me back.

"I'm ready to talk. But not details."

"Of course," I answered. In fact, discussing the details of trauma could cause more harm than good. Asking questions, or having a patient relive the experience, can re-traumatize them, worsening their condition. Patients needed to be in a safe space, with full control, under the watchful eye of a trained therapist before discussing the details.

"My dad beat me. He'd beat the shit out of me. It happened every day."

I sat, listening.

"It's not his fault, though, you know? He didn't know how to be a dad. You know that school down south? He was taken there. He didn't get to see his family again. And I know they beat him too. But I wanted to kill him. He died years ago, before I got a chance."

The tears poured out. Drew started crying, then sobbing. I waited until he was able to speak again. "There are a lot of people I would have killed if I had it in me. My hockey coach, he kept touching me too. It's why I don't like to have my clothes off."

"I'm so sorry that you've gone through so much." He nodded, drying his tears with a tissue.

"I gotta think about my kids, though. They're perfect. Sixteen and fourteen. They live with their mom. It's better that way, you know. Stop the cycle. Now they can't see me drinking." He pulled out their photos from his wallet.

"Your daughter has your dimples."

He winked at me, grinning. "She's a heartbreaker all right."

"Thank you for sharing your story with me." I acknowledged the sacredness of what he'd shared, grateful for the strength in his vulnerability, hopeful for him.

For some patients when they have a moderate amount of safety and stability in their lives, trauma therapy can be helpful in allowing them to regain a sense of normalcy. Trauma, like addiction, can be treated. Although much of the brain's learning happens in the early years, forming people's health and patterns of behavior, it turns out that you can actually teach an old dog new tricks. Brains learn until death, and they continue to form new circuits even in adulthood. Although trauma can shape a developing brain, it is not the end.

I explained this to Drew. I could tell he didn't believe me, but he was listening. Finally, he agreed to try it. I set him up with a trauma therapist on discharge. "Good luck," I said. He smiled at me.

I wrote up his discharge summary, cringing at the term "alcohol abuse." Those were two words that seemed miles apart for this patient. If anything, the alcohol was suppressing memories of abuse; it was trying to reduce trauma. Calling it alcohol abuse felt very deeply wrong. This is the reason we use medical terms. Drew suffered from abuse, and from it developed an alcohol use disorder.

A few months later, I was checking my email at the end of the day. There was a name that sounded vaguely familiar in the inbox. It was from the therapist Drew had been seeing, with his permission. It was a photo of a handwritten note. "Six months sober. Thanks for the help. There was also a photo of Drew smiling at the camera, dimples and all. I smiled to myself, packed up my stuff, and headed home. The sun was setting, and the sight was beautiful. I felt like singing.

4

Harm Reduction

I WAS INSIDE ONE of the harm-reduction shelters, setting up for the day. Harm-reduction shelters are set up to accept patients who are actively using substances or intoxicated. Many shelters bar people for using substances, and there are usually enough shelter beds available for people who are sober. Those who are intoxicated, however, are often at higher risk to the elements. They may try to start a fire for warmth and burn themselves, or pass out in a snowbank and develop frostbite or worse, freeze to death. People who are intoxicated are also vulnerable to violence, often unable to protect themselves.

One of the shelter staff, a colleague, came to ask me if I could see another staff member named Breanne* in clinic. Breanne worked at the shelter as front-line staff. Like many staff in resource-stretched shelters she was underpaid and had a big heart. Usually staff go to their own family doctor or urgent care, but I was okay to just take a quick look if it was something simple. A couple of staff in yellow vests escorted in Breanne between them. She was limping, and when she pulled up her pant leg, it showed an area that promised to be a spectacular bruise eventually. I felt the bones, and nothing seemed broken, so I encouraged her to see her family doctor later that day. "What happened?"

Why I Help People Take Drugs

"It was the building next door." I nodded, comprehending.

A few months earlier, a condo complex had gone up for sale, having been built over the past year. It was billed as luxury apartments. People bought the condos sight unseen, without realizing it was next door to an intox homeless shelter. Then they moved in. Unable to get their money back, raging against the injustice of having poverty so visible to them, they had taken to harassing the patients and staff. The previous week, someone had thrown a full beer can from the topmost floor of the tower at a patient. It ricocheted off the ground and hit her on the rebound. Had it hit her on the way down, it would likely have killed her. Breanne had gotten hit by a rock, again dropped from the top, again rebounded into her leg. We called the police, who took a statement.

This level of stigma that my patients face is on the more extreme side, but it is not uncommon. Between situations like that and the constant daily stream of "get a job," "take a bath," and the side glances and rolled eyes, my patients know what society thinks of them. In marriage they say that you need seven positive interactions for every negative one to build a healthy and trusting relationship. What about the relationship between people who are homeless and the rest of society? Do they receive seven positive interactions for every negative one?

Once when I was in Vancouver working at Insite, a patient came in with burns all over his face and his hands. He had stumbled several blocks before coming in, passing a clinic and an urgent care center. Some kids had thought it would be funny to light his beard on fire while he was semi-conscious and intoxicated. He stumbled to the one place he felt safe, the supervised consumption site. We dressed his wounds and convinced him he needed to go to the hospital. He came to us first, because he was afraid, and rightfully so. The supervised consumption site (SCS), the only place he interacted with people without addictions in a positive way, was the place he felt safest. This is the side effect of harm reduction— the power of grace. At Insite, people feel like they are met where they're at. They are given value, and people genuinely care whether or not they survive, regardless of their position in society. This grace offered is a powerful force. It helps people decide they are going to try not to share needles because they've realized they do have worth. When we keep bringing people back from overdoses, it gives them hope for a story beyond the one they are living.

At its core, harm reduction is evidence-based medicine that seeks to reduce harms associated with risky behaviors. It is part of the standard practice of medicine and commonly used in public health as well as in addiction medicine.

Despite this, harm reduction has become a loaded political term. When we switched from a federal liberal government to a conservative one, harm reduction was removed from policy as one of the pillars with which to fight addiction. When we switched from a New Democratic Party provincial government to a United Conservative Party one, several of the programs that were keeping people alive through the opioid crisis were shut down. I'm not advocating for any one political party or even one side of the political spectrum, and I don't think that my fiscal views really play a big role in the conversation. But it is difficult to see medical interventions become politicized. I think the reason for this is that, just like with the pandemic, everyone has an opinion and the science is not trusted.

As a doctor, it is my job to do the best I can with the facts that I know. And the evidence for harm reduction is overwhelmingly positive. Supervised consumption sites reduce overdose deaths. Sterile supplies reduce disease transmission. Intox shelters reduce frostbite injuries. Housing first models reduce lengthy hospital stays. All forms of harm reduction studied so far save taxpayers money—often for every dollar spent, $6–10 dollars are saved with harm-reduction initiatives. All sides of politics should be on board with this. However, there is a certain amount of stigma that we as a society have toward the use of certain substances, which we cannot seem to overcome. I have heard it said that this is related to the historical church's denials of self-pleasure. People should not use substances just to feel good. They become a burden to society and to taxpayers. Using substances for pleasure is a poor life choice.

Pleasure is not worth the cost to others. But there is a hypocrisy evident here.

When my good friend insists on going skiing every bluebird day of winter, I can at least breathe a bit easier knowing that she is wearing a helmet and skiing at a resort, a supervised site of her activity. She is choosing this inherently harmful and unnecessary activity just because it feels good to her. The pleasure of the wind in her hair, the powder under her skis, and the sun over the mountaintops—this is her primary reason for skiing. But skiing is a risky endeavor. I spent part of my medical school training in the mountains. The volume of injuries increased every year when the ski resorts opened. Still, if she breaks a leg, I will expect she gets good care in emergency despite her poor life choices to slide down a mountain on two expensive sticks. I will expect that she will get surgery as soon as is necessary for her medical condition, regardless of her decision to seek pleasure at the cost of the taxpayer. Instead of giving her money to the poor, she chose to spend the exorbitant resort rates for her own pleasure, and now society is paying for her decision. I will still anticipate that the surgeon who fixes her leg will let her know when it is safe to return to skiing, so she can continue burdening us all, and we can continue loving her anyway.

I write this facetiously to make the point that what society deems acceptable does not necessarily follow a moral logic. To be Christian means we answer to a higher power than the laws of society. Certainly, we obey the laws, but we strive to see the world through the eyes of a fair and just God, recognizing that human laws are often unjust. Christians through the ages have spent time in jail, breaking laws, and receiving unjust punishments, starting with Jesus and continuing today. It's uncomfortable to me that immorality is starting to blur with criminality. Using drugs may be criminal, but is it immoral? Is the pursuit of pleasure morally wrong when it applies to drugs but not when it applies to skiing? I'm not so sure anymore. These questions are more complex the deeper we dive into them.

Fortunately for the skiers, harm reduction has a basis in the pre-existing structures of society. As much as laws have been zealously enforced, grace has been interwoven into some of those laws. Seat belts have been made mandatory, recognizing that not everyone will drive well, and seat belts save lives. Bicycle helmets are mandatory for kids. Bars, which are supervised consumption sites for alcohol, are given rules they must follow including when to cut people off and what time they are allowed to operate. Alcohol is legal, meaning it is now regulated, quality tested, and people tend to not go blind from it anymore. Patients with high cholesterol due to diet are still treated for heart disease. Patients with type 2 diabetes who continue to consume sugar are treated with insulin. Harm reduction recognizes an inherent desire for humans to experience the fullness of life despite its risks, and it tries to keep them safe regardless of how they go about it.

The act of harm reduction, as it applies to substance use disorders, brings me to tears every time I think about it. When I hand a patient a bag of sterile needles and injection supplies, the action speaks louder than words. It tells them that I think they are worth taking care of, worth taking the extra step to ensure they don't contract HIV or Hepatitis C or any other blood-borne illness. It means I believe that they have a life worth continuing to live, and a future story ahead of them. I haven't given up on them, and I want them to take care of themselves. When a patient decides to rummage through their bag and use a sterile needle instead of someone else's used one, they are wrestling with their withdrawals, with the risk of offending the other person, and with the risk of not getting their drugs in time, just to try and make this small decision to choose hope for themselves. God is present in both of these actions. In every small decision that points to hope, to life, and to worth, love is gaining footholds.

I have seen that God is present in the supervised consumption sites, acting through the nurses as they bring people back, breathing life into them. God is present in the distribution of safe supply, in the prayers of those who hope that the uncontaminated drugs will keep patients alive until their addiction can be treated. God is present among the patients who, at the end of the month, share their alcohol with their friends at the cost of increasing their own withdrawals, so that nobody has to drink mouthwash or hand sanitizer to avoid having a withdrawal seizure. All of these are small moments where the presence of God is tangibly visible. You just have to look to find him.

One slow night, I was alone in the injection room at Insite while the other nurse was on break. A guy came in who I'd never seen before—his record showed he had been to Insite a few times but wasn't a regular. He took some supplies and then headed to his booth to shoot up.

    I noticed he had two hits, or doses, of heroin, and asked him if he was planning to shoot up both or just start with one and see how he did on it. He mumbled that he'd be careful, but just then, a girl in another booth started screaming. She was hallucinating, and walking around with an uncapped needle, endangering the lives of people around her. I gently approached her, calmed her down, and got her to put the needle away. It took a few minutes of talking to avert the crisis, but she was okay. I turned to do my systematic sweep across the injection booths—making sure everyone was still breathing. Panic hit as I realized the guy I'd just been talking to had shot up both hits at once and was face-down on the table. I yelled for help while dragging him off the chair onto the ground, terrified by how completely limp he was. He was a shade of blue-gray that I'd never seen human flesh turn. Other patients stopped shooting up and circled me—suddenly sobered by the blatant death in front of them, knowing it could have been any of them. I grabbed oxygen and our emergency kit, put in an airway, and started bagging the guy, medically alone in my first code as a nurse. Just then the staff worker came up to help—she had called an ambulance. She was new, and if it was scary for me as a medical professional it was even scarier for her. She tried to bag the man as I drew up Narcan, the antidote to his drug, but she wasn't able to make a seal with the mask over his face and she panicked. In that crisis moment, I realized that it was up to me to save this man's life. I froze in fear for a split second, utterly alone.

HARM REDUCTION

Then I felt a warm clear presence wash over me—something other than me, something more sure of itself. I believe that the Holy Spirit revealed his presence to me in that moment.

Suddenly calm, as though it wasn't even me speaking, words came from my mouth to gently encourage the girl working with me to reseal the mask. I drew up some Narcan and administered it. I broke the glass vial because my hands were shaking, but simply opened another, a reminder that God was using me despite my ineptitude. By the time paramedics arrived, the man was breathing on his own again. Now God has been in the business of saving lives using healthcare professionals for a long time. That night, he used me. That man came back a couple of weeks later to thank us. I wish I could say that he decided to quit forever, but I don't know. I do know that he lived, and because of that, there is hope for him.

Supervised consumption sites have saved the lives of every person who has overdosed in them to date. In every one of the thirty-plus peer-reviewed studies published *in reputable medical journals like the British Medical Journal, Canadian Medical Association Journal, The Lancet*, the *American Journal of Public Health*, and the like, supervised consumption sites have been shown to be successful at meeting their objectives. The area around Insite has been shown to have slower rates of increase in opioid deaths compared to other areas of Vancouver during this opioid crisis. There has been a reduction in overall public disorder around the site, including a significant reduction in public drug use. So why do supervised consumption sites exist? The formal answer is to increase access to healthcare and addiction services, reduce overdose related deaths, reduce transmission of blood-borne illnesses and other injection-related infections, and to improve public order. The research shows that it's done all of these and done them well. That's a big deal. I believe that this is a testament to the power of love. Because on the surface, supervised consumption may be a cold medical transaction of sterile needles; to anyone who has spent a day doing it, it is clearly much, much more.

Grace, the foundation of the gospel, the message that God has tried and tried again to hammer into our heads, grace is the core of what happens at supervised consumption sites.

Because the reality is, we are saved by Christ's love for us, not by anything we do to earn the love. And the same way, we are called to display that love for others, not because they earn it but because God loves them. We believe that grace alone has inherently transformative power. Because Christians know about the transformative power of grace, we can understand why harm reduction works. The people who work in this field are often living out grace in a way that should feel familiar to us as Christians.

A friend of mine from church named Mark* came over a while ago, asking to talk. Mark was frustrated because one of his siblings would not stop using drugs, and it was hurting the family. They were ready to cut off contact with his brother for good. His parents had spent so much money on trying to convince this brother to go to treatment. They had bought airfare numerous times to fly him out to various treatment centers in the States, telling him that if he loved them, he would attend. The whole family had sat the brother down for interventions. He would say everything he could to please them, then go right back to using substances. He had recently overdosed in their home, and paramedics had to revive him. They felt helpless.

Hearing the story, I understood the depth of pain that addiction had caused this family. The brother was deep in the current, and the family could not understand why he couldn't swim back to them. Not wanting to disappoint them, he told them what they wanted to hear. His inability to follow through made him a liar in their eyes. They could not comprehend the control that addiction had over this man.

Slowly, I started to explain how addiction works. I explained that very good people will say and do things that nobody would expect, because their brains have been rewired to believe that the substance is needed for survival. I described what to expect, and how to support this patient while maintaining boundaries—both my friend's boundaries and the patient's boundaries. Guilt often compounds trauma, and the pain of hurting people you love while not feeling able to comply with their wishes often leads to increased substance use.

Extending grace did not mean lending more money, or enabling the patient. It meant understanding his limits and recognizing what could and couldn't be expected of him. It meant loving him no matter what he said, and trying to avoid putting him in situations that would make him worse. It meant prioritizing keeping him alive because there could be no more to his story if he died. It was the exact approach that harm reduction provides.

This makes sense. Harm reduction is what it claims to be—it is essentially about reducing harm. It is an active process, to do something in the face of harm. It's not just handing out needles—it is a posture that communicates hope, that the patient will live, will survive, will thrive. It is one of love, of belief that there is more to this patient's story than the substances.

The alternative to harm reduction is to not reduce harm. This is a passive process, a stance of inaction. Some people see this as acceptable, to not be involved in somebody else's problems. It reminds me of the story of the good Samaritan. Many people passed by the person in the ditch. It was not their problem. This is not where the story in Scripture leads us. Jesus points out that the problem is not the man lying sick in the ditch. The problem is within the hearts of those who passed by—with their assumptions about him, with their inaction. Others see the harms that addiction cause as punitive, a well-deserved form of justice for bad decisions. The problem is, death is not a punishment, and harms do not deter this illness. Often the consequences of illicit substance use are unjust and disproportionate. Remember, by definition, addiction includes use despite negative consequences because of lack of control. Idly watching these harms happen to others with self-righteous pleasure is not a holy posture.

Understanding these concepts, Mark realized that inaction was not something he could stomach. He asked for teaching on how to use naloxone kits, on how to recognize and revive somebody who has overdosed. He joined Al-Anon, a support group for people who love someone with addiction. And he discussed setting boundaries with his family. Regardless of whether he chose to continue his relationship with his brother, in his own heart, he was able to heal some of the frustrations that a misunderstanding of addiction had caused. And this made all the difference for him.

It is my hope that as a society we start to love people with addiction as our brothers and sisters, choosing love and choosing action. This requires also choosing to actively reduce the harms they face in the hopes that we can keep them alive long enough to see how the rest of their stories might go. I believe that harm reduction is a critical part of any approach to treating addiction, and that as a society, we must include harm reduction in all of our interventions. This is how we start incorporating both grace and justice into our posture toward addiction.

ND# 5

Justice

"We will have to have security escort you in."

I was so nervous, butterflies in my stomach, at my first large speaking engagement. I had been invited by a seminary in Calgary to deliver a lecture on harm reduction and how I saw God in my work. Public speaking made me want to throw up, but I kept my mind on the content of the lecture and my passion for my work was calming. Until I was informed I'd need security.

Apparently there had been some threats and staff were not taking any chances. Hearing about the positives of harm reduction felt like injustice for some people, and that had created fear. This fear led itself to aggression. Still, I had published an article on harm reduction in *Christian Week*, and it had made waves. I'd received my fair share of angry comments, but nothing threatening. Security seemed like overkill.

I took a breath and thought it over. Accepting the presence of security seemed like a small price to pay to be able to speak freely on a university campus. I set aside my protests, repressed my anxiety, and walked to the front. As I started, I saw tensions melt. People listened well to what I was saying. We had a good academic discussion, and everything stayed civilized. To listen to one another, and to seek to understand, is just as much a part of human nature as to fear and to threaten. I believe that this positive part of our natures best reflects the heart of God as he embodies the mysterious connection between justice and grace.

I recently signed a work contract, something I typically just scribble on and hope for the best. I tend to not read legalese well because I don't understand it—so I sign and trust that the fine print is fair. It has been explained to me that this is a bad idea. One lawyer friend used the phrase "incredibly stupid." The thing is, I just haven't bothered to learn the terms. So for this contract, I decided I would try to be responsible, and actually read the thing. It started out by defining the terms of the contract. As I read, I started to learn a new language—as each word was defined, I learned its meaning. I realized that sometimes in order to create understanding, we need to define our terms well.

So let's talk about my understanding of the term "justice." Justice is a reflection of God's desire to rebuild the connections we have broken between each other, between us and God, and between us and the land. It is a way of piecing back that which we in our sinful natures continue to seek to separate. Justice is God's way of setting boundaries and not allowing us to ruin things further. Justice is inherently a gracious act, to give us stability and security and make the world an ordered place for our own well-being. As a Christian, I am bound by God's justice. As a society, we have also aimed for laws that support justice. In our flawed humanity, we don't always get it right. God's justice is not always the same as our worldly justice system. We still submit to our own country's justice system, but this does not mean forgetting the justice of God.

One of my personal characteristics is that I care deeply about injustice. If I saw someone being bullied on the schoolyard, or I read stories about people starving, or I saw an animal being mistreated—I feel these things deeply. It has been an identifying characteristic of mine ever since I can remember. My desire for justice is often much stronger than my desire for kindness, or my desire for grace for those perpetrating injustice. Some people naturally lean toward understanding. Not me. I lack tact. This is why I have had to work so hard to understand grace. To me, grace doesn't make sense, it feels unnatural. I am eager for justice, much more than I am eager to understand. And I think I am not alone in this. Sometimes in our God-given zeal for justice, we as a society miss out on understanding. The more we seek to learn about our laws and where they came from, the more we can understand how best to apply them today.

I recently went for a walk with a good friend of mine named Brian. We've been friends since high school, and he was helping me hobble around with a sprained ankle this summer. I had a rough childhood, and he was someone who has helped me more fully become myself—walking alongside me through all the ups and downs. Brian is a close friend and was even my grad date; we have always been platonic friends and he is happily married. He has encouraged my successes and been there for me along the way, and we have the security that a long-term friendship provides. I think about Brian, and I realize with a pang that he wouldn't exist if our laws against opioids were successful. This may seem like a leap, but bear with me. Brian's parents are both faithful Christians and are active members of their church. Brian's dad is of European descent. His mom is of Chinese descent. This union was illegal not so long ago in Canada. Anti-Asian sentiment has made a comeback with the advent of COVID-19, but it has been festering under the surface for many years.

As Canada was becoming a nation, Anti-Asian sentiment was common across North America, and the fear of Chinese people marrying white people was a real thing. So much so that laws were created to isolate and stigmatize Chinese people further. I get a shock when I think that these laws were created because the Canadian government didn't want people like Brian to exist. Half-Chinese, half-white people were not wanted in Canada.

Sir John A. MacDonald, Canada's first prime minister, stated in the House of Commons:

Why I Help People Take Drugs

> If you look around the world you will see that the Aryan races will not wholesomely amalgamate with the Africans or the Asiatics. It is not to be desired that they should come; that we should have a mongrel race; that the Aryan character of the future of British America should be destroyed by a cross or crosses of that kind.... Although the Chinese were invited at first, for very obvious reasons, in the paucity of labor and the sparseness of population in California, when they were valuable as working machines for a time, they soon began to crowd in there, to be formidable there, and they would swarm over into California, and if they were allowed in British Columbia, they would swarm over there in large numbers, and we would have an Asiatic population, alien in spirit, alien in feeling, alien in everything, and after they attained formidable proportions in their numbers, you could not keep them out.[1]

Benjamin Perrin, a law professor at UBC (and a Christian as well), sums up the situation of the day in his book *Overdose*:

> On September 7, 1907, rabid anti-Chinese sentiment in Vancouver reached a flashpoint with three days of anti-Asian riots. It began with a parade organized by the "Asiatic Exclusion League," starting at City Hall then proceeding to Chinatown. Twelve-foot-wide banners bore slogans that read "Stand for a White Canada" and "We have fought for the Empire and are ready to fight again." The mob smashed windows and storefronts throughout Chinatown and the Japanese quarters, with several reports of violence against people.
>
> Responding to the 1907 Vancouver riots, the federal government sent William Lyon Mackenzie King, who was then deputy minister of labour but would later become a Liberal prime minister, to investigate. Even though it wasn't in his initial mandate, King wrote a thirteen-page report on the "Need for Suppression of the Opium Traffic in Canada." It's hardly the stuff of any policy justification I've ever seen: it reproduces his correspondence with the Anti-Opium League, mentions a visit to an opium den

---

1. "Official Report of the Debates," 1589.

and his own over-the-counter purchase, discusses how other countries were dealing with the issue, and includes some newspaper clippings. King argued that prohibition should be national policy and promised it would completely stop the use of opium. He appealed to the moral panic that opium use was causing among white people, particularly concerning young white women....

In short, the case for criminalizing opioids in Canada in the early 1900s didn't rest on concerns for public health and safety, nor was it founded on any scientific or medical evidence. It was politically motivated, based solely on racism and appeals to moral rectitude.

"Smoking opium was not considered to be physically harmful or socially degenerate," writes Robert Solomon, a professor with the University of Western Ontario Faculty of Law who has researched drug prohibition in Canada. "Yet the public strongly disapproved of opium smoking among whites, because it involved mixing of the races—a matter considered far more serious than the drug's effects.... This crusade succeeded because it was directed against Chinese opium smokers and Chinese opium factories, but at the same time posed no threat to the larger number of predominantly middle-class and middle-aged Caucasian users who were addicted to the products of the established pharmaceutical industry."

At the turn of the twentieth century, morphine, heroin, and cocaine were unregulated; they were even found in such products as teething medicine for children, toothpaste, and cough syrup. In fact, as Dr. Scott MacDonald from the Crosstown Clinic pointed out, the word "heroin" was the marketing name given by pharmaceutical company Bayer for its "heroic cough suppressant" that contained the narcotic at the time.

King's report was the launching pad for a national policy of drug prohibition that would criminalize illicit drugs across Canada, with increasingly severe sentences for both users and traffickers. The promise was to eliminate illicit opioid use. More than 110 years later, that promise remains a failure.[2]

2. Perrin, *Overdose*, 127–32.

Why I Help People Take Drugs

Brian wouldn't exist if our laws against opioids were successful, because the laws against opioids were written to prevent Chinese people and Caucasian people from having kids together. Laws should not be tossed aside just because they were racistly implemented. But when under scrutiny, the laws don't hold up to science or medicine, they started with racism, and they only serve to cause further harm. It's time to take a hard look at why we hold onto them so strongly. In this case, the tradition that these laws are steeped in is tainted with racist hatred.

I do occasionally drink alcohol, because after all, Jesus's first miracle was turning water into wine. Still, I hold to the several teachings in Scripture that advise against public intoxication. I think it would be a bad idea for me to get blackout drunk, and I don't think this is in God's plan for me. But would I support criminalizing alcohol? No. I don't think that moral codes should equal criminal codes when it doesn't cause harm to others. For example, I definitely think drinking and driving should be illegal. But drinking at home alone? Morally maybe not a good thing, but not deserving of jail either. This is also the approach I take to tobacco, opioids, stimulants, and other drugs. Yes, smoking cigarettes is bad for you. Yes, it can make you sick with cancer or COPD. Yes, it can harm others with secondhand smoke. No, I'm not going to smoke personally. No, you shouldn't be allowed to smoke in schools. No, smoking in your own house shouldn't mean you go to jail.

So why are we so adamant that smoking opioids is any different? The science suggests that prohibition doesn't work—it creates a harmful toxic supply instead. Reports of moonshine blinding people played significant roles in the re-legalization of alcohol. Enough people drank illegal alcohol that people started to realize the lives lost to moonshine actually mattered. Have enough people died of fentanyl for us to realize that we should start to go back to the way things were and consider legalization?

If you had asked me, before this career, whether or not drugs should be legalized, I would have told you "obviously not." Drugs are bad. It only makes sense that they should be illegal. But presence among people who use drugs has changed my mind. These

JUSTICE

are people who love, who laugh, and in whose faces I see the image of Jesus. Their lives are sacred. They do not deserve to die in these numbers because we deny them a safe supply of drugs while we treat their addictions. I have come to change my mind on this issue—I believe that prohibition is not the answer. Treating addiction, healing trauma, and saving lives of people who use drugs by supervising consumption and intervening in overdoses—this is the work of the Lord. I can say with conviction that he is present in these spaces, helping reduce the harm that the evil in this world does to the lives of people. I believe that one day we will live in a world where the appeal of drugs is not needed because people are so wrapped in love that drugs have lost all meaning. I do not live in that world right now, though, and all I can do is help join in the presence of a loving God who cares for people as they are. Presence has helped me realize that justice does not mean criminalization. It means compassion and healing.

So there I was, at a harm-reduction building in the downtown eastside of Vancouver. I was working for an agency that provided housing for patients who required long hospital stays for IV antibiotics, but who wouldn't stay in the hospital because their addiction was too strong. The community transitional space was provided so we could care for their infections with lower barriers than the hospital provided. I was hooking up this participant to her IV antibiotics in her room while looking at her sleeping, broken face. It was covered in bruises and swollen after her recent assault. Jasmine* had been through a lot. I bent over her, leaning against the bed to get to the IV site, when all of a sudden I felt something brush against my thigh. I'm standing there, two sterile connector pieces in my hands, thinking, "Okay, first connect the IV, then figure out what's touching you." I'm amazed that I had the mental capacity to take the extra split second to connect that IV—it's probably my greatest act of self-control to date. So I connect the thing, then I look down. Worst fears are realized. There is a *rat* on her bed. I start screaming at the top of my lungs while leaping back from the bed. "Get up there is a *rat* in your *bed, get up now!*" She sits bolt upright, realizes why I'm screaming, rolls her eyes, glares at me, and grumbles, "His name is *Patches*!" Then she rolled over and went back to sleep.

What the heck! This thing had a name?? It was a fitting name, 'cause it was missing fur in lots of places. But it was disgusting. God has endless grace. I do not. I kept yelling. There was no way I was gonna be in that room with a rat. Who knows what it was carrying. I saw rats all the time in the Downtown Eastside. Half the time, they're eating human feces. Rats on beds are *not* okay.

Jasmine sat up, told me to calm down, picked up the rat, and started stroking it. I gagged, but sat down. Another rat scampered past my leg, she picked it up too. Oh, great, she's got two rats as pets in her room. I consciously tried to slow my breathing and told her that rats carry lots of disease and we cannot have them running free in the room. She glared at me and said, "The day nurse was way more understanding." Well good for the day nurse. But then she shoved some papers into my hand, and I looked down at two veterinary certificates.

Apparently, she had refused to give up the rats, so the day nurse took her to the vet and paid to have the rats vaccinated and cleaned. Now that is a good person. That is a person who understood that this woman's love for her pets is the only love she experiences, so it is important to encourage. I am not that good a person, and I would never have thought of vaccinating the rats. I would have set out traps when she wasn't looking and told myself her heartbreak would be good in the long run when she didn't get rabies. But this other nurse understood something I didn't. Fortunately, the participant had grace for me. She let me calm down, and then made me hold one of the rats so I could get used to it. I mustered up all the courage I had in me, and asked its name. "Glock" she said. "What a weird name, how come you named it that?" She frowned, suddenly shy, and didn't say another word. I picked up her cue and understood that the conversation was over for now. So I put down the rat and told her I'd be back in half an hour to disconnect the IV.

Over the next few months, we grew a bond together. I put up with the rats, and she put up with me. We talked a lot, and even though I didn't swear often or know how to use a crack pipe, she decided I was all right. One day, rat in hand, she looked at me. "Wanna know why I named him Glock?" Sensing that something deep, something vulnerable was about to come out, I nodded. She told me about her beating—the one that got her into the transition beds in the first place. Her pimp had caught her keeping a $10 tip to herself, and decided to make an example of her to the other working girls. He and a bunch of his buddies gang raped her in a park at night, beating her all the while. Now she's pretty fierce when needed, so when she tried to fight back, they pulled a gun on her. A Glock pistol, to be exact. They raped her with the barrel, threatening to shoot her inside, beating her all the while. Finally, they left her barely hanging to life.

She had told the police, with the support of the nurses at the hospital who processed the rape kit. No charges were laid. She had substances in her system. A conviction would never stick.

I sat beside this strong-willed woman, and I wept with her in horror as she told me her story. When she was finished, I looked at her through my tears. "Why would you name your rat, this thing that you love, after such an awful experience?" Jasmine smiled at me. "Because, somehow, it needed to be redeemed. Because there's gotta be good out there, even if I don't see it." She pulled out a faded picture of Jesus from a desk drawer under her crack pipe, kissed it, and put it back.

Being invited into the depths of Jasmine's understanding of Jesus was like nothing I have experienced. It came about through patience, relationship, and both of us having grace for one another. To me, that moment showed how God works through people. Little ways of bringing hope into situations that only merit despair.

There is room for justice, and for the law, in the treatment of addiction. It just doesn't belong where you think it might, or on the timeline you might expect.

Why I Help People Take Drugs

"Don't go in there if you don't have to," my colleague warned me. She was a social worker with our hospital's addiction medicine team, and she wasn't prone to stigma. Her warning was a real one.

"Tyrell* steals. He stole a nurse's keys and wallet. He steals everything that isn't pinned down. Plan to lose the stuff in your pockets if you go in there."

She was right. I emptied all my pockets and headed in to meet Tyrell. During our interview, he denied all illicit use. I looked around the room as we talked. Piles of jewelry stolen from the neighboring mall, clothing with security tags attached, and women's purses were stashed in all the corners. His urine drug screens were positive for fentanyl and meth. This was his way of supporting the habit.

The problem is, Tyrell had a deep tissue and bone infection, and was going to be in the hospital for several months. This could not continue.

"You're going to get caught," I warned, a few weeks in once we'd built up a relationship. He just looked at me.

"I spent years in and out of jail, since I was eleven. That's where I got this infection." Doing some quick mental math I realized that Tyrell had spent more of his life in jail than out of it. In the medical field, we describe the personality traits that come from this as being "highly institutionalized." He couldn't stop stealing because he had no faith that we would be able to treat his pain, and he needed to have access to drugs in order to stay in the hospital. Tyrell couldn't be honest with us because he'd fallen into that trap before—telling jailers the truth and then getting in more trouble. For him, the hospitalization was just another jail stint.

Over time, our team built rapport with Tyrell (still always emptying our pockets before entering the room). And over time, he stopped stealing as much. The piles of stuff in his room reduced, until one day a few months later I walked into the room and the only thing he had was photos of his family, and a beautiful blanket that had been quilted by his sister.

Tyrell also agreed, a few months in, to be started on opioid agonist therapy to treat his opioid use disorder. When I write this, he is still in the hospital, but his plan is to move out of town on discharge and go stay with his family who are all sober. He wants to maintain sobriety.

Had we focused on the injustice of his thefts at the beginning, we would not have been able to build the rapport that would curb his behaviors. That quick jump to enacting justice is often too fast for people to adapt to. The criticism of this might be that he continued to steal, to harm others, for a much longer time. In response to this, I would suggest that, practically speaking, jail time hadn't made the problem better, but had made it worse. Building rapport as an intervention to stop thievery was effective and was faster than sending him back to jail only for him to continue this behavior the next time he was in the hospital.

We are often faced with difficult situations as healthcare providers. Was this man's consistent thievery worth discharging him from the hospital over, knowing he would die without treatment? Was it worth sending him back to jail, knowing that extended jail time had already disrupted his ability to engage with society?

My experiences have taught me that real justice is often disguised, and that the structures we have set up in society to promote justice are sometimes imperfect. Justice is a complicated thing and really only God can provide it in its fairest forms. We must still strive to improve the systems of society, as a means of seeking out justice. Still, truest justice comes from God, and it is difficult to enact societal justice without trying to follow his deep love for all people.

6

Treatment

"I need to quit."

Brad* was sitting in the room, shaky but determined. Before I could even introduce myself, he'd stated his purpose.

"Okay, well you're in the right place. I'm Dr. Meera, and I'm one of the doctors at the addiction medicine clinic here. Why don't you tell me a bit about what's going on?"

"Every time I'm drunk, I do stupid shit. I'm not who I want to be. I drink every day now."

"Okay, and how long has this been going on for?"

"The past year with COVID. I can't control my anger. I'm getting worse and worse. I lost my job, there's nothing left to do but drink now. I think about dying every day, jumping in front of a train. But I couldn't do that to my kids. I don't see them anymore, but I know they care about me."

"How much do you drink every day?"

"I started with a drink or two, but I'm up to twenty-six ounces daily. When I wake up, I shake really badly. I have to drink to stop the shakes."

We talked for a while, and Brad started opening up more and more. I gave him my spiel on addiction being a chronic illness, on the loss of control associated with it. He shook his head.

TREATMENT

"The drinking might be out of my control, but that's not the worst part. I hit my wife when she dumped out my vodka. That's not how I grew up. I don't want to be that guy. I could have stopped it, I know I didn't have to. But I did it."

Brad started crying. Shame poured out of his eyes and ran down his cheeks.

Bit by bit, the story came out. He was now staying at a friend's house, his wife had kicked him out. He couldn't bring himself to tell anyone what had happened. He didn't know if his wife had told anyone either.

"I have to stop drinking. I have to learn to do better." The steely determined look returned to his face.

Plenty of my patients are at the stage where they want to stop using substances. The tricky part is getting them access to addiction treatments.

Once the body has gotten used to a certain substance being around often, it adapts its functioning to work around the substance. Suddenly stopping the substance "cold turkey" can lead to withdrawal symptoms. With alcohol, for example, stopping drinking suddenly can lead to seizures, delirium, and death.

Alcohol works on certain neurotransmitter pathways in the brain. The oversimplified way that I explain this to patients and to med students, is as follows:

Alcohol slows down the workings of the brain. It slows down neuronal function, motor function, cognitive function, etc. It's a little like driving with one foot on the brake. But if you have enough alcohol on board, for long enough, the brain starts to adapt. Brains adapt slowly, because they don't want to be jumping around for every little thing, but when they adapt, they do a good job. The brain always wants to return to homeostasis, or its baseline. So it tries to speed things up. Soon enough, you find yourself driving around with one foot on the gas AND one foot on the brake. Now let's say you drive around like this for a year. Then one day, you stop drinking. Your foot comes off the brake. The problem is, the brain takes a while to notice and to release the foot from the accelerator completely. In that time, neural activity increases significantly. Muscles are in overdrive, causing tremors. Neuronal hyperactivity can lead to seizures or delirium. This is what we call withdrawal. It takes a while for the body to ease off the accelerator enough to guarantee safety. It takes even longer for it to figure out how to function again without alcohol.

To help prevent withdrawal from being a life-ending decision, medical supervision is needed for certain types of withdrawal. We monitor a patient's vital signs and withdrawal symptoms, and we treat them with medication to help prevent seizures. These medications are dangerous in and of themselves, and can be addictive or toxic in high doses. If the patient relapses and drinks with the medications on board, they can die. Hence, the medical recommendation for supervised withdrawal.

So where can you go for supervised withdrawal? In Calgary, there are three detoxes that are publicly funded to various degrees, at the time of this writing. To get into detox, you have to line up first thing in the morning, with other people who are also trying to get in. You wait in a room with all of them, watching them shake, retch, and sniffle their way through withdrawal. You try to manage your own nausea and shaking. Each of you is called to speak one-on-one with the nurse. He or she gets the story, gets the vital signs, and writes down some notes. Then you return to the room to wait. Once everyone's seen the nurse, often hours later, the decision is announced. Only five of the most severely ill people might be admitted that day. The rest of the room will need to try again tomorrow.

In the meantime, those patients may need to return to their substance. It's a terrible feeling, telling somebody who is begging for sobriety that they need to drink again tonight in order to stay safe and try again in the morning.

"Please, I don't want to go back to shelters. I don't want to overdose."

"Please, isn't there anything you can do? If I go home I'll drink and I'm worried I won't come back in the morning."

"Please, I'm ready to stop. I don't want to keep using."

These phrases enter the hearts of the detox admission nurses, but they can't magically create more beds.

One of the detox admission nurses told me a story from when he received a call from a family doctor in the community.

"Are you the one in charge of deciding who gets in?"

"Yes, I'm the admissions nurse."

"Well, I wanted you to know that because of you, my patient died yesterday."

"What?!"

"He tried to get into Renfrew, and you guys wouldn't take him, so he killed himself."

The nurse looked through the files, trying to remember the patient. The patient had actually come three days in a row. The first two days, he didn't make it in. On the third day, he was accepted for admission. Instead, he gave up his spot for a woman next to him, who had recently been assaulted. He was asked if he was sure, but he declined the spot. Later that day, he died by suicide.

Trying to explain the situation to a grieving doctor was hard. Having to keep making those decisions was even harder. There was simply no more room at the inn. The nurse went home that day and cried. The helplessness overwhelmed him—to be privy to the lives and stories of patients, and to have to refuse them help. He cried for days. He was stuck in an impossible situation, playing God with the lives of the patients. He couldn't have done anything differently.

If you are one of the lucky ones who makes it into detox, you would be placed in a room with several other people in withdrawal. With limited privacy, everyone's vomits are audible. Shaking, sweating, droves of people curled up on cots, praying for it to be over. Meals, nurses getting blood pressures, and physicians writing prescriptions, provide breaks in the day. This lasts about five to seven days for those who can take it. Many leave partway through detox. They aren't allowed cigarettes, coffee, or cell phones. There are a few books and a few games in the common room. Near the end of the detox, there are addiction counselors available to discuss next steps.

Once the worst of the withdrawals are over, it's time to discuss the treatment options.

There are several inpatient treatment centers in Alberta. A few of these are public facilities, but several are private. Many do not use evidence-based treatments, instead choosing self-help guidance or untested group therapies. There is a lack of regulation of treatment centers in our province. Some are for profit. A few will require that patients go off their psychiatric or addiction treatment medications in order to attend. Others will accept patients on those treatments, only to convince them to go off of them once they've gotten going. A handful seek to be evidence-based in their psychotherapy and in their medication therapy. All of them work for some people, but none of them work for everyone. They involve stays of between twenty-one days and a year, with a variety of assistance provided after graduation. Getting into any of them is difficult, as they're all full nearly all of the time. The wait list is weeks if you're lucky, months if you're not.

After detox, patients are often forced to return to the same situations that they were in before detox. Most people who are homeless return to shelters, where they typically relapse. If the treatment centers can't get a hold of them, they lose their treatment date. People who are housed return to their homes, to throw out their drugs and dump the alcohol down the drain. Most of them relapse too. Some attend outpatient treatment in the meantime, trying to stay sober. They go to AA meetings or SMART recovery, or they attend counseling or medical appointments. Those who are well-resourced stand the best chance at maintaining sobriety while they wait for a treatment date. Not everyone is interested in inpatient treatment, and some manage to attain sobriety with outpatient therapy. The more resources a person has to help them remain sober as an outpatient, the better their chances of success.

When the call comes with a treatment date, people typically must return to detox and try to get in, five to seven days before their treatment date. This timing is critical—if they don't get in, they may not have completed their withdrawal, and the treatment date might get pushed back. If they get in too early, they hold up a bed that someone else needs, or they go home and risk relapse before the treatment date. Having a treatment date is taken into consideration when triaging detox admissions, because of the importance of getting people to treatment.

Treatment centers are highly structured, with schedules, urine tests, chores, and other patients. The expectation is that patients give it their all. In return, they receive a sober community of people who are ready to support them. Not everyone can manage this, and some leave part way. Addiction treatment is largely unsuccessful if there are significant cognitive deficits, psychiatric illnesses, or impulse-control issues. The problem is that all of these things also increase the likelihood of relapse and poor outcomes.

Once people leave treatment centers, they are still at high risk for relapse. With opioids, if they are not on pharmacotherapy, they're actually at a higher risk for death because their tolerance may have lowered significantly. Treatment without medication is medically contraindicated for opioid use disorder for this reason. Lots of community supports are required to help patients integrate into their neighborhoods. They may need help with housing, or with food preparation. They may need assistance with social skills, or basic home maintenance. Something as small as having a fruit fly infestation might cause patients to move out and return to shelters, because they don't know what to do and are overwhelmed. Many struggle with anxiety and fight an uphill battle when trying to rebuild their lives. They don't know who to turn to for support, and are afraid of judgment. The long-term chronic effects of addiction become more invisible, but ever present, as people move forward in sobriety, fearing what will happen if their colleagues or friends find out who they used to be.

When teaching new physicians about addiction medicine, I find it tricky to explain the art of medicine. It's difficult to follow a clear structured plan. Medicine is about adapting everything we know about science and the human body to meet the complex needs of people. This means that we have to do our best to assess all the factors affecting someone before determining what the best treatment for them is. For example, if I have a patient who is stable on methadone, has been sober for several years, is married and has a family, and is a connected member of their church, I am not going to be handing them a paper bag full of sterile needles for their own personal use. I am going to be supporting them in their goal of sobriety. But since I know that relapse is a part of the journey of battling this chronic illness, I will still make sure that at every check-in they are aware of how to live through a relapse—how to access an SCS, where to get sterile supplies, etc. We will have a good relapse prevention plan in place.

Not everybody aims for sobriety, however. Recovery, for many people, can look like slightly increased control over their substance use, or goals for improvement of health, or return to employment. Recovery has also become a politicized term, used to mean abstinence or bust. This is medically inaccurate. Each person determines what recovery looks like for them. Some will aim for what they feel is more attainable, knowing themselves and understanding that they need several small wins before being able to imagine bigger ones. Some will need to be encouraged toward making small steps, such as going to the hospital to get an infection checked out. Each step, no matter how small, requires a huge effort from the person to believe in themselves, and to care for themselves. Each step is therefore a celebration for all those rooting for the patient. Hearing the news that a patient regained visitation with their kids is enough to set our whole office cheering some days.

The barriers that people face when trying to get help are unacceptable. For a society that claims to be anti-drug, we don't do much to help treat people with addictions. The resulting burnout for people who work with patients who are addicted is understandably huge. I have to face a patient like the one who was in my office, and tell him what the road ahead entails. I have to manage his expectations for immediate sobriety, and help him access resources to keep him getting by. I have to be the one to tell him he needs to keep drinking for the night before he can attempt detox in the morning.

For Brad, after I explained the next steps, he stared at me in disbelief. "Can't I just go to a hospital or something?"

TREATMENT

If we sent all of our patients who require withdrawal management to the hospital, our emergencies and hospital beds would be overrun. We cannot, unless they are very, very sick, send patients to the hospital for this.

"Okay, but can't you just give me some meds to take home so I don't have to drink tonight?"

And therein lies the situation that most physicians find themselves in. Do I give this patient the medications, knowing there is a risk they might relapse and die because of it? Do I go against the medical guidelines that make outpatient management contraindicated in this patient? Or do I tell the patient to keep drinking, and erode his faith in his ability to quit?

Many physicians will choose to give their patients meds to take, reasoning that their job is complete as long as they've warned the patient of the risk. If the patient "chooses" to relapse, and has adverse effects, that's on them. Some physicians will tell their patients to keep drinking, with the hopes that the patient will taper their alcohol and still keep trying. Some will try to advocate for a hospital admission if there are any spare beds. The reality is, there is no good option available if detox is full. Physicians too are stuck with providing substandard care. This frustration often works its way out on the patients themselves. They are seen as "blocking" beds in the emergency room, or as "drug seeking."

This is how we define structurally vulnerable populations. They are vulnerable because ultimately, the responsibility for being a square peg trying to fit into a round hole always seems to land on their shoulders. Societal structures are what make it so that patients can't get access to treatment. Yet at the end of the day, the doctors and nurses go home to their beds, while the patients are the ones who are left figuring out what comes next. This is the reality that our patients face every day. It makes every small step of self-care a miracle, and each decision toward health a step of recovery. My patients have such resilience in the face of hardships that many people will never know. They won't know, because they aren't walking alongside, looking, noticing, and advocating. It is my hope that in reading this, these patients will be seen, that you will be motivated to walk alongside, to hear the stories, to provide a safe space to share.

We were in our morning team rounds, and the social workers and addiction counsellors were discussing a case. "I don't know if she'll get to keep the baby." Silence filled the room.

Chloe* had been one of our patients off and on for a while. She'd found out she was pregnant early on, and had tried hard to stop smoking meth and fentanyl. She had a few admissions where her urine drug screen tested positive in the first few months, but since then had seemed to be aiming for sobriety. She had gone to detox, jumped through the hoops, and made it to treatment. In the past three months she had found housing and had made a place for her baby. She was determined to parent her child.

Still, the odds were against her. Her positive urine drug tests during early pregnancy suggested that her stability was tenuous. Normally, patients in this situation have their children apprehended by Child and Family Services. At least now attempts are made to place the kids with family members as kinship care, or keep the kids within their cultural identity. This hasn't been the case for very long. As part of a government-led anglicizing of patients who are Indigenous, kids were taken from their homes. The Sixties Scoop, as it was called, took newborns from their parents and placed them in foster care, primarily in European homes. Their biological parents were judged based on European standards—for example, not having a fridge in the home because food was stored differently in Indigenous communities, could lead to a charge of child neglect. Many kids were brought up without recognition of their culture and without formal Indigenous status.

Chloe didn't want anyone else to parent her child. She had seen what that could do. She was adamant. So during her pregnancy she did everything and anything she could to set herself up for success. She worked harder than I've ever seen at therapy, meetings, and sobriety. She took her anti-craving medications without ever missing a dose.

TREATMENT

Now all that was left to do was wait. Would it be enough?

After rounds, I went to see her. She was sitting up in bed, her baby in the bassinet beside her. She smiled at me.

"She's perfect," I said.

"I know," she replied, beaming.

Resisting the temptation to wake the baby by cuddling her, I instead turned to Chloe.

"Have you thought of a backup plan?"

Her face darkened. "My grandma can take her. I want to keep her, though," she added fiercely.

"I know. I hope you get to."

I wrote my consult note. I used terms like "immense success" and "highly motivated for abstinence from drugs." I wrote that I strongly supported this new mom getting to take her baby home. I wrote that I felt sure the baby would be safe with her mom.

Finally, it was decided. Chloe was going home with her daughter. At rounds the next day when the news was announced, everyone cheered. She had worked so hard.

Still, it was with some doubts. Child and Family Services would continue to check in on this new family, offering supports while keeping an eye on the situation. The decision lacked the permanence that would make us all breathe a little easier. This was fair, though, because substance use disorders are a chronic illness, and relapse was always a looming possibility.

A few months later, one of our team's social workers came into the office, beaming. "I got to hold Chloe's baby today!" She was doing really well with motherhood, fighting her own self-doubt to do right by her daughter. She had maintained her sobriety, and her whole world had become about taking care of her daughter. Her sponsor lived a block away, and her grandma lived next door. She was surrounded by people who cared about her.

Child and Family Services would stay on a couple more months, and then sign off. A new season had begun in her life. There was hope.

7

Bad Medicine

On my days in the hospital, I work with patients who have been admitted with critical illnesses, who require assistance managing their substance use or withdrawal.

It was on a day like this that a consult came in for a patient I knew named Josh*. I took a quick scan of the chart. Admitting diagnosis was febrile neutropenia—a lack of immune system combined with a sign of infection. Oxygen levels were low, and a lung X-ray looked cloudy where it should have been clear. The patient was HIV+, Hep C+, and had several other viral co-infections. Not receiving treatment. Only place where he connected with healthcare was the supervised consumption site (SCS). He used meth and opioids. The consult was because he was withdrawing from opioids and wanting to leave the hospital. I had a resident with me, a learner. He came back from seeing the patient and said that he didn't look like he was in withdrawal. I asked which patient we were discussing. The resident had forgotten it, remembering the patient by his bed number, "B5."

"Please do not refer to patients by their bed numbers. Tell me his name." The resident checked the chart and wrote down the name, embarrassed.

I told the resident to actually ask Josh the withdrawal questions, not just guess from a distance. He did, and came back with a much higher withdrawal score.

The emergency room nurse who gave the medication was exhausted, likely pulled in from another unit to support COVID. She dosed his opioids, then reported his heart rate dropped although his respiratory rate stayed the same. Despite this not being a side effect of opioids, she decided to hold his medication. Josh went into further withdrawal.

The diagnosis for his pneumonia was likely PJP, a form of pneumonia common in untreated HIV positive cases. We needed to rule out tuberculosis, however, as Josh was homeless and Indigenous, both of which increased his risk for TB. He slept outside which made the risk of TB low, but it was still a possibility. To diagnose TB you need three samples. He had two in the hospital, before leaving. Josh told the ER nurse it wasn't just that his withdrawal was being undertreated, it was also that he felt "institutionalized." The negative pressure room brought up too many triggers for him. This could have been jail, it could have been isolation while at residential school, it could have been many things. He couldn't stay.

I called public health after hearing that Josh had left. The public health doc in charge of vulnerable populations during COVID understood my fear for the patient. She called the supervised consumption site, and approved them to collect the third TB sample outdoors. The SCS was able to collect it. He then used while there, trying to cope with the trauma. He overdosed, and it was a bad one. They had to use several vials of naloxone to revive him.

Josh declined to come back to the hospital; he was so afraid. They convinced him that he would not need the airborne isolation rooms anymore because they had ruled out TB. He came back.

The doctor who admitted him called me, wanting to increase his opioids so he wasn't in withdrawal. "As high as you can without him crashing" was my advice. We had to do whatever we could to try to keep him there, so we could treat his acute illness. Josh was likely to die without this. The SCS staff promised to visit him every day.

In the middle of the night, Josh left again. Four days later, he still hadn't re-presented. I stayed up late, waking up between fitful sleeps, wondering about him, praying.

This is a patient who was articulate enough to know how his history had impacted his care. He had the capacity to make decisions for himself, and that autonomy had clearly been taken away from him previously.

My week in the hospital was up for this rotation and I was back to shelter medicine. I called to check in midway through the week. Josh had returned! He was doing much better. I asked about him a few weeks later and heard he got into a harm-reduction building for patients who are HIV positive. He was housed, was on antiretroviral medications, and was in recovery. He was still using substances at the SCS, but was now much more connected to the community. It was a miracle.

Having been in this field from a medical standpoint for many years, both as a nurse and as a physician, I've been privy to the unique failures that medicine has offered my patients. This started before my time, but has carried through to today.

From touting oxycontin as a cure-all, to naming pain as a fifth vital sign, physicians are complicit in the development of today's opioid crisis. Physicians have shaped social expectations around pain, reporting pain as unacceptable, and medicating it. Although this may have been well-intentioned, we now know that pain is expected, and that trying to numb all pain carries great risks. Several of my patients' opioid use disorders developed after being prescribed long-term opioids. In fairness, most physicians were unaware of how addictive opioids could be. Evidence is now being brought to light that several drug companies falsified information and lied about the addictive nature of opioids. Physicians refused to believe their patients and stuck by the drug company claims, insisting that the addictive nature lay within the person, not the drug itself.

Regardless of intent, overprescribing of opioids worsened the state for patients with chronic pain, driving some to develop opioid use disorders. Chronic pain is a complex topic that is a bit outside the scope of this book. However, the basics of chronic pain are that it involves a malfunctioning of the nervous system to continually report pain when there is no response available to ease the pain. Ideally, pain acts as a waving flag, alerting the body to realizing that a limb is broken, or a hand has been inadvertently placed on a hot stove. For painful chronic conditions like arthritis, the pain can be debilitating, creating a vicious cycle where pain prevents exercise, causing weakening muscles, and worsening the arthritis. Patients feel they are advocating for themselves, when urging physicians to start or increase their opioid doses, to treat chronic pain. Opioids treat pain well, but temporarily. They nearly always produce tolerance, requiring more and more to produce the same effect on pain. This eventually leads to conflict with physicians. Patients start to be labeled as drug seeking. They ask for early refills of medications because they used it more than prescribed. They report using it for pain flares, but don't realize the pain flares coincide with a bad day or a fight with a spouse. Soon, the opioids are being used to numb emotional pain, which is linked to physical pain. Combined with tensions with the medical system, conditions are prime for the development of an opioid use disorder.

Part of this is due to the way we understand pain. In North American society, pain is not an accepted part of life. It is expected that pain is an indicator that something is wrong, or something must be done. Inability to tolerate a baseline level of pain comes with privilege, but it isn't always good for us. Many patients with chronic pain, who are unable to accept that their lives will include pain, report higher pain scores than patients who are accepting of this. Treatment for chronic pain ideally should not include opioids. Opioids will work, initially. This is why the appeal is there to take them. But the reality is, opioids are not indicated for chronic non-cancer pain. They cause more harm than good. Other non-opioid medications, while often less effective initially, can help with chronic pain. The most effective treatment for chronic pain that has been shown to lower pain scores is a combination of psychotherapy and physiotherapy. These wrap-around treatments, provided by a few chronic pain clinics, are resource intensive and don't often have patient buy-in. Wait times are lengthy, and patients who are unable to cope with the idea that they may have to live with pain end up back on opioids.

Physicians, in wrestling with patients who are opioid-dependent and have chronic pain are often at a loss for what to do. They may force the patients to taper, without knowledge of how to taper effectively. Opioid tapers, when done slowly enough that the brain does not notice, have actually been shown to improve patients' pain once they're finally off the opioids. This is partly because chronic opioid use ironically causes hyperalgesia, which is an increased sensation of pain. But patient buy-in is required for this, and it needs to be done carefully. When opioids are tapered rapidly or discontinued, patients are put at high risk for buying illicit opioids, and for death by overdose due to this.

So some patients end up on low doses of opioids for life. Physicians might force patients to sign an opioid contract, in order to keep prescribing. These contracts frame the issue as a moral one, asking patients to give their word they will not use opioids differently than as prescribed. This is not helpful except in identifying the diagnosis of opioid use disorder. Contracts often cause a further erosion of the therapeutic relationship between physician and patient. Prescribing opioids works for a while, until the patients require more and more. Some patients become elderly on opioids, and people who are elderly metabolize opioids differently. They are put at risk of falls, fractures, and other adverse effects. Opioids contribute to death in geriatric patients at an alarming rate. This struggle is the inevitable result of being dependent on opioids for chronic pain. Still, for some, this is the only path they can tolerate. These patients should be maintained on their opioids, without increase, but without taper until they are ready. Education—for both physicians and patients—is the way to protect these patients from developing an opioid use disorder. Because once fentanyl is in the mix, there is no easy way back. The potency differences are so great that a return to just prescription strength will no longer be effective.

Just as many physicians did not receive education on the intersection between chronic pain and opioid use disorder, many have also not received education on addiction medicine itself. Addiction medicine was created as a specialty by physicians who believed that addiction was an illness, not a moral failing, and who believed there was hope for treatment. The first physician to publish this was American Founding Father Benjamin Rush in 1784, who also signed the Declaration of Independence. He spoke out about addiction being a chronic illness that could be treated by medical interventions. Despite this, addiction continues to commonly been seen as a failure of willpower and not deserving of treatment. The physicians that started addiction medicine also started the research behind it, paving the way for today's researchers as they seek newer and more effective treatments for each substance. Excellent evidence exists for addiction medicine treatments so far, although much more research is still needed.

Still, addiction medicine is only just starting to be taught in medical schools. Many practicing physicians do not know how to treat opioid use disorder, despite the death rates surrounding them from the opioid crisis. Patients with substance use disorders are labeled problem patients and are avoided rather than sought out.

Opioid use disorder has treatments that are currently available. These treatments are changing as fast as the drug supply, and my description of medications in this book will likely be outdated by the time it is published. Despite this, it is helpful to know that there are very effective medications already available and addiction medicine is growing as a field.

One available therapy is a medication called buprenorphine-naloxone, or Suboxone (brand name). The naloxone in it reverses opioid toxicity when injected but is not absorbed when taken by mouth. Buprenorphine-naloxone is a tab absorbed through the mouth, so the naloxone in it just acts to prevent the medication from being injected. Buprenorphine is the key ingredient, and it too is an opioid—just a safer one. In most adults, buprenorphine has a ceiling effect for respiratory depression. This means that taking too much doesn't lead to overdose deaths—it may make you sleepy, but typically doesn't cause overdose unless there are other factors like liver disease or concurrent benzodiazepines or alcohol. When patients are on a stable dose of buprenorphine, it is harder although not impossible for them to overdose when using illicit drugs. It also helps reduce cravings, which helps patients whose goal is abstinence to maintain sobriety. Other medications such as methadone or slow-release oral morphine can also help patients to maintain abstinence. We do have similar medications for alcohol use disorder, but only recently have they become covered by drug plans in Alberta. Unfortunately, we don't have similar treatments for stimulant use disorder yet. Funding research for this has been difficult.

Buprenorphine-naloxone is a life-saving medication for many who struggle with opioid use disorder. It is literally a pill that reduces the risk of death by overdose. No special license is needed to prescribe buprenorphine in Alberta, but despite this, many physicians still don't. Training is available free of charge online for physicians who want to learn—but many don't access it. This is mind-blowing. As I write this, we are in the middle of an opioid crisis and a COVID pandemic, with more people dying from opioids than COVID, and yet still many primary care physicians have not taken it upon themselves to learn how to prescribe this life-saving treatment for opioid use disorder.

A big part of the reason for this is funding. Physicians are not paid for taking extra training to prescribe a medication. Many physicians in Alberta are paid per patient—meaning that patients who require more time, or may not show up, are considered financial liabilities in a practice. In countries with privatized healthcare, this issue is much worse. There is no financial incentive for physicians to seek out training in buprenorphine-naloxone, and the patients who require it are often considered problem patients. Another reason physicians don't seek out extra training is the perception of substance use disorders as a moral failing not a medically treatable illness. Physicians have not been taught about buprenorphine in school until recently. It is perceived as a niche medication, despite concerted efforts from the Canadian Medical Association to ensure that all physicians are comfortable with it. If it were a treatment that family physicians could prescribe for COVID, everyone would know about it, and most physicians would be seeking out information to get comfortable. But opioid use disorder has not had the same airtime, even among doctors, that COVID has had. This is another way that the structure of medicine contributes to the stigmatization of patients with substance use disorders.

Stigma is often discussed in the soft skills part of medical school. This is disappointing, because we are seeing a massive widespread amount of death fueled by stigma. Not only our failure to recognize or attempt to stem the flow of deaths due to the opioid crisis, but also the deaths due to racism. Consider people like Brian Sinclair or Joyce Echaquan, both Indigenous patients, who died in the hospital due to racism by hospital staff who did not assess them properly and presumed they were intoxicated or drug-seeking. These are the stories whose names I can write about, who hit the media. They are not the only stories, though.

I was walking through a COVID ward in the hospital, on my way to see a patient who was COVID-positive and had an addiction. Addiction medicine had been consulted to help manage her withdrawals. She was certified under the public health act, meaning that security stood outside her door to prevent her from leaving impulsively in her drive to use substances because she forgot she had COVID. I had increased her dose of morphine and was checking in to make sure it was enough, that she wasn't having any cravings. If she needed more, I was happy to provide it—the morphine treated her withdrawal, kept her from using illicit substances and overdosing, and kept her from leaving the hospital and potentially spreading COVID to more people.

As I left her room, I heard a shout. "We need help in here!" Running toward the commotion, I saw several people in yellow isolation gowns converging on one room. The attending doctor was already in the room. I was relieved—I wasn't needed. When you first start medical school, you do things like crane your neck

Why I Help People Take Drugs

at car accidents, wondering if you'll be needed to help, or listen eagerly for overhead pages asking if there is a doctor on the plane. Once you've been practicing a little while, all that foolishness disappears. You dread the page on the plane, hoping to just have a quiet flight where you don't have to work. You breathe a sigh of relief when you see EMS already attending a car crash—you won't need to pull over and offer help. Codes in the hospital are a bit like that. Of course you run toward, you get things started, offer help. But when the code team arrives, you gratefully hand over care, thankful that this is now someone else's role who can do a better job than you can.

The patient in the room was screaming inhumanly, punctuated with swearing and threats. Through the sea of yellow gowns and face shields, I could see his back arching on the bed, security trying to hold him, arms and legs being tied by nurses with restraints. The screaming was aerosolizing his COVID, putting everyone at risk. Another nurse gowned up, hurrying but trying to stay safe, follow procedure, sanitizing her hands between each step. She brought in a needle with a sedative, injecting the patient. Slowly, the scene changed. People trickled out of the room, removing their gowns, their gloves, wiping their brows. The patient mumbled, semi-conscious, moving slowly. The attending doctor came out of the room.

"You okay?" I asked.

"Yeah. I don't know how you deal with these guys. I'm going to consult your team."

As the days passed, we learned more about this patient. His name was Bill*, and he typically slept outdoors, without accessing shelters, and without accessing any form of healthcare. He had gotten COVID from another person he'd let into his tent on a particularly cold night. The voices in his head told him not to trust anyone in authority, to be afraid—common elements of psychosis. Bill used substances constantly, anything he could get his hands on, just to try to get them to shut up—to find peace. Even as he progressively got sicker, he would not consider going to a hospital. One day, he was found by someone walking their dog, unconscious on the side of the path. EMS was called, and he was brought to the hospital. COVID had attacked his lungs, lowering his oxygen levels, making him unable to breathe. He was admitted to the COVID ward.

As Bill started to improve, the fear and the voices kicked in. He tried to leave. Security stopped him, and he fought with every survival instinct he had. He was pinned down and strapped to the bed.

Our team tried hard to engage with Bill during his stay. We brought him food, journals, and set up a TV in his room. We worked hard to build rapport with him. We asked about his substance use, but he wouldn't tell us much. We tried to convince him to take medication to help with the withdrawals, or at least to help with the voices, all to no avail. Bill wouldn't tell us why he didn't access care other than "I don't like doctors." We spent as much time with him as we could, to try and ease the suffering of his forced stay with our presence. At the end of his required isolation, the minute he could, he left without saying goodbye.

I don't know what kind of trauma this patient had faced in healthcare prior to this stay. All we could do was try our best to love him with the limitations we all faced, but it wasn't enough to overcome his fears, his trauma, and his mental illness. I saw in his chart that Bill had previously been treated by a psychiatrist who had later been convicted for sexually assaulting other patients. Was that the reason he hated doctors? I didn't know.

What I know is that the reality of caring for patients with addiction is that it is sometimes exceedingly difficult. Hospital beds are limited, and resources are stretched thin. Some days all we can do as doctors and nurses is to struggle to complete the bare minimum that our jobs require, staying late to finish charting, worrying that we are missing family dinner night. We can't spend time thinking about how the structures of our society need to change to help us deliver better care to our patients, because we don't have that extra time.

The failure of medicine is not in any individual's medical practice. It's that we aren't able to address the failures of society too. The ways that medicine fails patients reflects the ways that society fails them. Society doesn't want to fund psychotherapy, extra detox spaces, or training for healthcare workers. Money flows to socially acceptable things like a new cancer center instead. Healthcare workers speak up sometimes, but it's not mainstream, and it largely goes unheard. The real complicity of medicine is that we are not standing up and loudly saying that addiction is a medical not a criminal issue, and that we can treat it if given the chance.

Even with the stress that we are under, I think it is still possible for healthcare workers to seek out ways to better care for this population. My friend who motivated me to write this book called me at the beginning of the pandemic. "How's the book coming along?" I tried to explain to him that I was working long hours, constantly on call, afraid for my life with this new disease, trying to protect my patients, and looking up how to write a will. He compassionately heard all of my fears and listened to my concerns. "Okay, but I know you can find five minutes every day. This book matters too." At first I didn't believe him. He couldn't possibly understand what we healthcare workers were going through. But with every opioid death, I thought about the book, and felt a pang of guilt. Soon, I realized, I was going to have to find a way. I structured writing time into my life, in the middle of a dual opioid and COVID pandemic. I can't believe I did it, but here I am, writing. It's helped me understand that it doesn't have to be one big thing—each of us is able to find a way to advocate in small portions in our lives.

Whether that means chipping away at the opioid trainings available online, or spending five extra minutes with a patient who struggles with addiction, or simply giving some of the money we earn back to agencies who help the patients we struggle to care for, we are capable of doing better for our patients with addiction.

The other thing in medicine that I think we healthcare providers tend to forget is that healing is not limited to people who have graduated from medical school or a nursing program. Most overdoses are reversed by a fellow person who uses drugs. This is why naloxone kit distribution has been so helpful. People who use drugs form their own safe communities and try their best to take care of one another. This happens as a by-product of presence—when you use drugs, you are most commonly around other people who use drugs, so the deepest relationships are formed there. Many people who use drugs learn intently how to use a naloxone kit, because they know it may save their best friend or their partner. Knowing how to use a naloxone kit is like knowing CPR—it's important not for your own life, but so you can save somebody else. Carrying one around is an act of selflessness.

Overmedicalizing the act of healing someone is a common problem in our society. Overdose prevention sites, where people can use drugs safely while someone is there to revive them if they overdose, do not need to be only medically staffed. Giving naloxone is actually relatively easy—anyone can do it. So when we medicalize these sites, requiring things like a healthcare number or ID in order to access them like a hospital, we create barriers. It means that patients who don't have ID or aren't willing to reveal their identity can't access lifesaving supports. It won't prevent them from using drugs; it just prevents them from coming back from an overdose. It callously turns a sterile medical eye away from the value of their lives. Initiatives like this are often well-intentioned, trying to force people into the medical system so they can more easily access treatment. Again, these initiatives lack the wisdom of presence. Those staff members and patients who are present on the ground, kneeling and watching people die by overdose—their wisdom is what should be listened to. The voices of people with active substance use are the least heard and least believed in medicine, and this is the biggest failure of medicine itself. All paths forward must include the voices of the people who they are about.

"Your next patient is here."

I went out to the waiting room. "Doug*?"

Another patient answered. "He's outside having a smoke."

The receptionist went outside looking for the patient but he was nowhere to be seen. I went back to my room and waited, finishing up my charting from the last patient.

Why I Help People Take Drugs

The appointment time came and went. Finally, Doug came back in. Luckily, I was available. I went out to the front to get him.

He came in, hands black, contrasting the rest of his skin. A classic sign of someone who sleeps outside and burns charcoal or wood for heat. Sitting in the chair bent over, he wouldn't look at me.

"What brings you in today, Doug?"

Slowly, he started talking, staring at his shoes.

"I hit a boulder going 70 miles an hour on my bike. I think I broke my neck. It happened two years ago. I passed out and some people dragged me to their camp and took care of me. I can't really use my hand since then. And I can't raise my head."

I realized that Doug was bent over because he couldn't straighten his neck. Nowhere in medical school did I learn how to take care of an untreated broken neck where the person had survived for two years without medical care. He had been cared for by peers, other homeless people living outside. They had done a good job of keeping him alive. He told me he couldn't walk for at least a month afterwards.

Well, I said to myself, let's start with the basics. I had Doug take off his shirt so I could better visualize his spine.

It took a while. He had two jackets, four sweatshirts, and two T-shirts. It was cold outside. I asked him when he last took off his shirt. He couldn't remember, but it was at least several days.

Doug's spine was prominently deformed at the level of his neck. His neck muscles bulged with the weight of holding up a broken spine that had healed in misalignment. "My neck muscles are sore."

No kidding, I thought to myself.

"I sometimes use fentanyl to help with the pain, but I try not to. Maybe once a week."

Doug was adamant that he did not want to go to the hospital. I sometimes find it difficult to explain to my acute care colleagues who think that they see everything in emergency rooms. There are some patients who are simply too afraid to access healthcare. In shelter, faced with a patient who refuses to go to the hospital, I have treated gunshot wounds, stabbings, and now, a broken neck. In Canada, we have universal healthcare. Cost was not the reason Doug didn't want to go to the hospital. It was, quite simply, fear of stigma.

He was willing to go with peer support to get an X-ray. It confirmed an old, misaligned fracture. The radiologist called me urgently, recommending spinal surgery consultation.

Doug was not ready yet. He just wanted to know whether or not it was broken. He panicked when I mentioned the words "spine surgeon." His timeline did not fit the timeline of ideal care in our system. He was marked down as "refusing care against medical advice."

So, we waited. Doug came to see me regularly. We built trust and rapport in the shelter. Finally, he asked if I knew any of the surgeons personally. I had met one of them, and felt I could call him to explain the situation. Doug agreed. His surgery is booked for next week. This is the power of outreach, and of respecting the timeline of my patient.

Healthcare that is patient centered requires an understanding of the patient's timelines, fears, and needs. It requires compassion. I believe that God uses healers, because healing is a part of the will of God in the world. Not only healing the sickness of addiction, but the sickness of our society that causes us to treat people with addiction so poorly. So part of my job as a doctor is to pray for a broken system that I am complicit in, that causes my patients such pain. When I pray over this daily and then approach my patients, it becomes harder to see them as the problem. It helps me understand that all I can do is ask for grace personally and try to be present for my patients as they struggle through a world that is callous to their needs.

8

Dogma

I'VE SPENT MY PAST few weeks crying alongside two of my closest friends. After trying for years to get pregnant, they had a miscarriage in the second trimester. The day after setting up the baby's room, they were in the hospital talking to the funeral home about the remains of their child.

I went to the hospital to see them, to try and be present in a time where there is nothing you can say so all you can do is be there. I walked past bassinets and the sound of crying babies to enter the room where my friends sat, empty-armed and pale-faced. The sun shone through the window, almost blinding, reflecting off the white hospital walls. We tried to drown out the cries of other laboring women as we talked.

There are no words to describe the devastation that the loss of a child has on a person.

I've been walking alongside this couple since then, spending quiet evenings at their home, surrounded by flowers. I've had glimpses into the pain without a full immersion—I go back to my own life at the end of the night. Still, I can't imagine responding in any way other than by trying to share as much of the grief as I can.

Grief creates a sacred space, a complex swirl of feelings that come in waves. It is both quiet and deafening. It is deeply intimate.

People are allowed into that space slowly and carefully. Any missteps in this warrant frantic apologies and the receiving of grace.

In this sacred space of contemplation, it is jarring to think of the blue and red lights of police, or to think of the clanging of bars, the click of the handcuffs. I can't imagine involving the police in the loss of a child, or a court of law. I can't imagine questioning if the mother was using substances, or blaming her for the death of the child.

And yet this happens to people who struggle with addiction in the United States.

Today I read an article about a twenty-one-year-old woman from Oklahoma who was convicted of manslaughter after having a miscarriage.[1] Brittney Poolaw was about as far along as my friend. She too delivered in a hospital. I imagine she would also have had to talk to a funeral home. When she got to the hospital, worried about her baby, she wanted to be as open with the healthcare workers as possible. She let them know she had used meth, hoping this information might save her child. The meth was not found to be a cause of death for the fetus; instead it was speculated by the medical examiner to have been a possibility alongside several other medical possibilities. Despite this, Brittney was arrested after going to the hospital. Her grief was processed in a jail cell, where she still sits. An abortion at her gestational age would have been legal. But admitting to drug use during pregnancy in the hopes that it would save her child landed this mother in jail.

The American Medical Association, which represents US doctors, spoke out. "Drug addiction is a disease amenable to treatment rather than a criminal activity."[2]

Brittney Poolaw was sentenced to four years in jail for manslaughter, in October 2021. The same month we lost our friends' child.

Approximately 1,200 similar cases have occurred in the past fifteen years.

1. Taylor et al., "Criminalisation of Miscarriage," 260–61.

2. American Medical Association, "Treatment Versus Criminalization," para. 1.

According to Dana Sussman, deputy executive director of the National Advocates of Pregnant Women, a pro-choice advocacy group, the recent explosion of similar criminal cases is part of the crossroads of America's War on Drugs and the personhood movement.

Both of these movements are spurred on by the church.

When I seek God in the situation with my good friends, I am left with many questions. I don't know why this happened to them. I know many people who are far less careful in pregnancy who have healthy deliveries, and some women who are very careful who miscarry. I know that God is the one who ultimately decides who lives and who dies, and there is so much out of the control of parents and doctors. I don't know why my friends' child died. I don't know why Brittney's child died. I still have faith that God is good, despite that bad things happen to good people in this broken world. But a huge part of this story reminds me of John 9, where people asked Jesus whose fault it was that a man was born blind, and he gently let them know they were asking the wrong questions.

As the church, we are asking the wrong questions about addiction.

We are asking questions like, "Why did you do that?" and, "Why don't you stop?"

We are asking questions like, "How can we punish this wrong?"

We ask, "How can I stay safe with so many people who are addicted in my neighborhood?"

And we come up with answers ourselves, without stopping to hear the voices of the people who struggle with addiction. The church is not listening to science, or to the medical professionals who are shouting that addiction is an illness. I would go so far as to say that large segments of the church are only listening to themselves at this point. But the problem is, God is not only found within the church. He works through all people, whether they are aware of it or not. And the church risks losing sight of him when he works in places they refuse to go.

I say this as part of the church. My faith informs every part of my work. I am a Christian first and a doctor second. Being a doctor allows me into the places where others don't get to go, to see God at work in intimate spaces of personal health.

What would happen if we asked these questions in the case of Brittney? "Where is God in this situation?" What if we trusted the doctors who were in that space with her, as they banded together with other doctors across the country to say that her addiction is a medical, treatable illness? To say that meth was not known to be the cause of this child's death?

What if we asked the question, "Why do people use drugs?" or, "Does criminalizing drug use help reduce drug use?"

What if we asked, "How can we help reduce drug use?"

What if we listened to the answers?

The church, when given power and a voice, is at high risk of losing the ability to see God. Scripture themes throughout the Old Testament and the New show a God who sides with the oppressed, who comes alongside those who are suffering, who chooses self-sacrifice over power. This is the God that Christians are asked to follow. His early followers did just that—they wrote letters from jails, were hanged for civil disobedience, chose to radically love all people instead of just those already in the fold.

I think another important question to ask is how are we reflecting Jesus? How do residential schools, and the deaths of thousands of children ripped away from their parents in the name of cultural erasing, reflect Jesus? Does defending the intent behind residential schools do this? Does criminalizing people who use drugs do this? Does jailing miscarrying mothers do this?

God has asked us to be a beacon on a hill, the salt in the food, to reflect who he is so that others may also come to know his love. He has asked us to set aside our own comfort, to give away our cloaks and turn our cheeks. He has asked us to give up all our money to follow him.

I would suggest that following God into the lives of people with addictions means giving up the war on them. It means keeping our eyes open to where God might be at work and setting aside any preconceived notions. It means seeking to know more about God through study of his word and his world. It isn't coincidence that I learned about God in the Downtown Eastside because I went to learn about God at Regent College. Science without theology, and theology without science, provide an incomplete view of the world. Both are needed.

It is embarrassing, at times, to be a Christian in the field of addiction medicine. I write this book with some trepidation, knowing my colleagues may find out just how Christian I am. I don't talk about my faith much at work other than superficially. It's going to be hard when it comes out that actually my whole reason for being is to be surrounded by the Trinity, seeking God in all the places I know he exists.

I walked into a patient's room in the hospital. The window beside him showed a grey sky with frost on the ledge. The room was cold and I shivered. The patient was sitting with one of our team's social workers already.

"Oops, sorry James*, I'll come back."

"No wait, it's okay, we're just finishing up."

I sat down, waiting for their visit to end.

"I will not go back there. They're part of the reason I'm here. No more Christian places." James was adamant. He was admitted with frostbite, and had partial amputations on both feet and one hand because of it.

"What happened?"

"I relapsed. I was doing so good and then this guy came by and he was giving away some extra meth . . . I just had a small puff; it wasn't much."

It was enough. He looked intoxicated and was kicked out of the Christian shelter on a bitterly cold night. What he didn't realize was that the meth also had some benzodiazepines mixed in, which kicked in after the meth wore off. He passed out on the street a block away from the shelter. He woke up hours later. His fingers and toes were black.

"Look, I know I messed up, and this is my fault. But if they had kept me inside, I'd still be able to walk." He teared up. The grief of losing a part of yourself after amputation is overwhelming. He was struggling to cope.

James had the option to try again at the Christian shelter, to eventually access their housing. But fear of losing his housing if he relapsed prevented him from wanting to work with that agency. And I couldn't blame him.

Looking down at his bandaged stumps, I felt so sad that Christians had not helped him. He would not access any Christian services anymore and wanted nothing to do with them. He needed shelter, and because he used substances, they had sent him out into the cold.

People have a hard time understanding Christianity or seeing it beyond the harm it's causing. The only Christian shelters in Calgary do not allow entry for patients who are intoxicated. Those patients are left to fend for themselves, trying to get into one of the crowded intox shelters, or sleeping outside and risking frostbite. Lots of ideas feed into this mentality—these patients could act differently, choosing God means not choosing drugs, and abstinence is the only way to recovery. These are all myths. The reality is, God is present whether you put Baileys in your coffee or fentanyl in your meth. God is present among people who are intoxicated but still manage to care for one another. God is present, lying at the feet of the intoxicated patient shivering in a snowbank in the cold after being kicked out of a Christian shelter for relapsing. Unhelpful and harmful. This is how Christians are seen in my field, because this is how Christians often visibly act in my field. The whole purpose of this book is to spur the imagination: What would happen if Christians chose differently?

Christian agencies in our field do help people who are homeless if they don't use substances. However, they often do not help people who are actively intoxicated, or people who are struggling to maintain sobriety. They may do good work, but they don't typically help the people that this book is about. I would also submit that there are many of us Christians who do good work with people who have addictions, but we don't do it corporately, as the church, through Christian ministries. We do it individually, as people who are trying to follow God. This is not the same thing. God clearly states throughout Scripture that faith is not meant to be only individual, but that he uses the church. We are meant to act as one body with many parts.

For this to happen, mainstream Christians need to consider these things en masse, and church leaders need to ask what their churches can do to help support people with addictions. Churches need to be willing to fund Christian parachurch ministries even if they don't have perfect stories of hope to produce at every fundraiser. Christian donors need to ask what programs and services are available for people to access who are actively intoxicated. And Christian ministries need to be willing to practice what Jesus preached, to interact and care for all people, not discriminating against people with illnesses.

Walking down the hospital hallway with a social worker, we chatted about our patient. He was dying of lung cancer due to smoking tobacco for several years. The cancer had spread to his brain, causing mood swings, vision problems, and loss of coordination. He was getting close to the end of his life. "He's a sweetheart," she said. "Did you know he's been married to his wife for forty-three years?"

I was in awe. Darren*, the patient, and Jolene*, his wife, lived in poverty, sharing a room with a stranger by hanging up a sheet between them. They had managed to stick together for forty-three years. My parents divorced early and I didn't know anybody who had stayed married that long. They were an inspiration to me.

Darren laughed at me when I told them how impressed I was. "You're young, you'll learn how to do this one day." She hit him with a napkin when he said: "I tried to leave her but she keeps clinging to me." Both of them laughed. "I'm just kidding, I'd be crazy to leave this woman. She's the love of my life."

As I got to know the couple, I learned that both had taken to smoking fentanyl relatively recently. They found it was a way to cope with their poverty, their aging, and their traumas. Neither wanted to continue. Jolene asked to be started on buprenorphine and then and there in the hospital I wrote her a prescription. Darren was on palliative pain medications and couldn't use buprenorphine.

Our social worker told me about the place that this couple stayed. There was no food in the house. It was dirty and crowded. People used drugs in the living room. Strangers walked in and out. It wasn't safe.

"We're working on it," she said. They were trying to find a new place for Jolene to live. She couldn't go back there. It was a long commute, and she had no money for the bus.

To maximize her time with Darren, our plan was for Jolene to stay at his bedside in the hospital. This was the standard of care for palliative patients—if they wanted, they could have a family member stay in the room so they wouldn't have to be alone. We would just let the staff know and it shouldn't be an issue. We provided meal vouchers for Jolene, so she could care for herself while caring for her husband.

As we left the unit, I walked over to the charge nurse. He had his head down, charting. "Hey, sorry to bother you. For Darren in room 24, his wife will be staying at the bedside. Can we provide a cot for her?"

He looked up, and made eye contact with me. Pointedly. "This isn't a homeless shelter." The words came, jarring me.

All the nurse could see was this patient's addiction. He couldn't see the forty-three years, the attempts to live life together, the grief of losing his physical abilities. He couldn't see that Jolene's presence was important. I looked at the cold, metal crucifix, dangling from his neck as he spoke. It felt distant, weaponized, threatening.

This is not the God that Scripture tells us about. As Christians, we have to be so careful to try to make sure we are not using the Lord's name in vain, associating him with things that do not belong to him.

I have been fortunate to have been invited to speak publicly about my work in harm reduction from a Christian perspective. Speaking at churches, seminaries, universities, and parachurch organizations, I've been able to meet many Christians from all walks of life. Most of the time, when people hear my stories, they come to understand that God works differently than they expected through the lives of people with addictions. Many people start asking what they can do to help, or how they can join in.

Some people, however, react to my stories of where I've seen God in the world with anger and hate. Once, after speaking at a parachurch organization in my own city, I was told by the board that I was no longer welcome because I was clearly working for Satan, not for Jesus. Despite my profession of faith in Jesus, I was seen as an outsider to Christendom, not to be trusted.

Another time, after a sermon, a man approached me at the front. People were chatting and the usual post-church buzz of activity was going on around us. I smiled at him, and he patted my hand. He then told me that if God had wanted this unholy message to spread, he would have made me prettier.

There is a deep ugliness in the church. We do not always listen with an open mind to what God might be asking of us. We react with anger or with fear that the way we do things may have to change. The church cannot hope for redemption without repentance. We must name the ways we have caused harm and practiced evil. We must grieve our incompetence and the damage we have done. We must ask for forgiveness from God. And we must stop the harm—we have to "go and sin no more" (John 8:11). We have to be willing to change.

What if the Christian agencies were the ones vying to open the supervised consumption sites, because the grace of caring for someone at their lowest is the best way to reflect Jesus? What if it was the Christian agencies that operated the intox shelters, who were the last to bar people, who were the ones who offered services without strings attached? What if the Christians were the best team players, who collaborated with the other agencies instead of duplicating services and slapping a "Christian" label on them? What if Christian groups funded research into medical treatments for addiction, trying to learn more about the world God has made? What if churches cared more for people who are marginalized than they did about increasing their own numbers?

DOGMA

What if the church channeled the desire for justice by funding lawyers to fight for people like Brittney Poolaw?

I think patients, communities, and medical professionals alike would do a double take in wonder at who this Jesus really was, who people would follow with such a willingness to change their own minds. This is the kind of miracle I hope for.

To be honest, the biggest problems that I see among Christians are the ones I see in myself. To understand this, I will share with you my worst story, the one I am most ashamed of. It comes from when I was early in the field, working as a shelter nurse.

I walked into the shelter, which was unusually quiet for an evening in winter. Stepping between the mats on the way to the medical room, someone called for me. "Hey! I need help! Please!"

I looked over. The guy laying on the mat clutching his stomach looked up at me. Tears tracked his face and he was bent over in pain.

I was stunned. He was the one that everyone on the street was talking about. New to the city, he had no respect for the street code that most of the patients who were homeless followed. He had killed two people that I'd heard of, without accountability because patients were unwilling to talk to the police and risk retribution. I had comforted at least four women that week alone who reported that he had raped them. No wonder the shelter was so quiet that night. Nobody wanted to come in while he was there. Just the previous day, I had visited one of my favorite patients in the ICU. His buddies reported that this guy was the one that had put him there, for trying to intervene when this guy was found raping someone.

All of these thoughts flashed through my mind as I looked into his eyes. "It's after hours. If you want help, go to a hospital." I said it coldly, and kept walking. "Please, miss! Please!" He called after me. I walked away without looking back.

I honestly did not care if this man lived or died. I was a nurse who was off duty at the time—I was just coming back to the shelter to drop off some supplies for the next day. I had no duty to provide medical care for him that day, and besides, telling him to go to a hospital was a reasonable approach. The reality is, I wanted him to die. I could not see any part of his humanity. All I could see was my favorite patient, connected to tubes in the ICU.

The next day, I came back to the shelter. He was gone. Relieved, I started my day. I felt a tiny bit guilty for how I had treated him, but I suppressed it. This man was not deserving of my care.

Later in the afternoon, the same man (Jason*) came stumbling back to the shelter, intoxicated. His stomach still hurt, and he needed blood work to determine if he had a bleed. I had been asked by the physician on that day to draw some. Without explaining the procedure, without any kindness at all, I sat him in the chair with the door open—I wasn't going to get assaulted in a room by myself with him. I tied a tourniquet on and pulled out my needle for the blood draw. He started crying loudly. "Please hold my hand," he cried. In front of everyone in the shelter, Jason broke and asked me to hold his hand. I could not believe what was happening, and I did not want to hold his hand. How dare he ask for help.

One of the male shelter staff came over, and held his hand, providing the patient with comfort and me with security. I drew the blood.

"Thank you. I'm so sorry. Thank you." He clung to me afterwards, like a child. The whole scene disgusted me. Yet I knew, I *knew*, that God called me to love him because he loved everyone. I could not cope with that idea. He was not human in my eyes.

Over time, I learned a bit more about this patient's story. He had experienced a lot of abuse as a child, and had witnessed several murders in his childhood. Slowly, reluctantly, he became humanized to me. I could see that he was an insecure coward, but I also could see how he had become that way. He was the worst sinner I knew, and he had no repentance in his heart.

Yet I also knew deep down that my reaction to him was wrong. It was justified, maybe, but inherently it was also wrong. Yes, he had caused unimaginable pain and ended several lives. The gravity of that did not change with me starting to see him as human. I started to develop empathy for Jason, from a distance. I was able to see that my lack of willingness to help him reflected my own inability to love, not his. Because love isn't earned, it's not deserved. It has nothing to do with the person you love, and everything to do with your ability to love unconditionally. Dehumanizing this patient meant refusing to see that his face bore the image of God, just like every other human. He had twisted it and corrupted it but it was still there. Even though I had accepted grace into my life, I was unwilling to extend it into his. "I'm nothing like that," I would think to myself, forgetting Jesus's tale about the man who gave thanks that he was so much better than everyone else.

I have never treated a patient that callously since that day, recognizing that there is always more to the story. Still, I cringe when I think about how little love I had for Jason. It has helped me to realize I am capable of hatred that takes me beyond my faith, and helped me to understand the depths of my own sin.

The deepest problem that Christians face is that we don't practice what we preach. This is inside me, and inside everybody I know. We forget about how much God loves us despite our flaws, and we look to others with judgment. Every time we catch ourselves doing this, we need to repent and to re-choose following God's way. This practice of repentance is the only way to remain the light on the hillside. When it comes to addiction, Christians have a lot to repent over. There is so much Christians don't know, again often due to lack of presence. There is so much more to the story that God sees.

And so I turn to God, again, and again. *My Father in heaven, whose name is holy. May I not use it in vain. May your kingdom reign and your will be done on earth as it is in heaven. Sustain me, and forgive my sins, as I forgive the sins of others. Deliver me from evil, and do not lead me into temptation. Who you are is true power and true glory, forever. Amen.*

9

Neighborhoods

"There's a new PSH building going up down the block." I paused, hearing this news from a colleague.

"Where exactly?"

"Well, put it this way. Your house is exactly halfway between it and the bottle depot."

PSH buildings, or Permanent Supportive Housing, are apartment buildings staffed by agencies with experience working with homeless and addicted populations. They are considered harm-reduction housing, so they don't kick out people who actively use drugs or drink alcohol. This is called "housing first," where patients are offered housing without strings attached. The evidence shows housing-first models lead to greater patient health, reduced substance use, reduced public substance use, and societal financial savings.

This particular building was going to have a room set aside for palliative patients—something we had been advocating for years for. Finally, there was somewhere people could go when they were dying. Some people were unable to beat their addiction at end of life, and needed to continue to use drugs until their death. Hospice would not allow this. So they ended up dying on mats in shelter, or outdoors. Now they would have a place to stay.

I am fully in support of housing first. The medicine, the evidence, the agencies—they all served to help. The problem was the location.

I had a quiet dinner that evening—just me and my hypocrisy, having dinner in silence. The building was just down the street. I had been working on the yard that day, making it nice, planting flowers and garden beds. I envisioned someone intoxicated, vomiting into my carrot bed, or passed out in the hedge. I envisioned used needles in the grass I worked so carefully to keep soft for bare feet.

This felt like an imposition of my work life into my personal sanctuary. I had spent years working with people who are homeless. Didn't I deserve a little time to myself? Didn't I deserve to not be bothered by "these people" in my own neighborhood?

Slowly, I started to process the information. I was filled with disappointment. There is no way I could maintain my integrity and do anything but support the building in the neighborhood. Along with this support came a bit of grief. It was the grief of realizing I'd been holding onto the sanctuary of my house and valuing it over the lives of people. It was the grief of realizing that I was being asked to give up my garden beds, to sacrifice my sanctuary at God's feet. And it was the grief of realizing that I too was guilty of the NIMBYism that I was so quick to point out in others. "NIMBY" is an acronym meaning "not in my backyard," a mentality that allows people to do whatever they want as long as they do it far away from me. It is self-focused and does not allow for hospitality.

So I made my choice. I would be supportive. I would adapt to what came my way. And I would choose to keep learning the lesson that every single aspect of my life belongs to God, not just my work life.

It's been a few years now, and my carrots have remained healthy and vomit-free. Nobody has fallen into the hedge, and although there has been an increase in litter, I've been able to clean it up. A few times, patients have walked by, spiking my introvert's anxiety each time. A couple times they've decided to come into the yard and chat. It's actually been quite lovely. Nobody has ever stolen anything from me. Everyone has stayed respectful.

The neighborhood I chose is the best neighborhood I know. I live in Bowness, a neighborhood known for its socioeconomic, demographic, and racial diversity. It's the kind of place where everyone fits in, where people roam the streets on unicycles and where kids trick-or-treat the same houses every year. Bowness has theft, for sure, and has a rough reputation. But it also has greatness in the way that the people embrace change while honoring tradition. Those of us who live in Bowness call ourselves Bownesians, comfortably easing into the perceptions of a cult. We try to eat local, shop local, and spend time with our neighbors.

Bowness is a neighborhood that is specifically designed to embrace people like our patients. Conformity is not an adjective that anyone would use to describe Bownesians. It is eclectic and fun. And yet even in this neighborhood, there are people like me who are reluctant to embrace people with addictions into our spaces.

Another similar neighborhood is located in downtown Calgary. A building was built to provide a one-stop shop for health services for vulnerable populations. It contained an urgent care center, a sexual health center, and harm-reduction supplies. Later, a supervised consumption site was opened on site.

Rhetoric surrounding the supervised consumption sites in Alberta changed with the changing of political parties. A media frenzy whipped up, using dehumanizing language and publishing articles referring to people with addictions as zombies. The government hosted several town halls where people could complain about the sites, then published these complaints and used it to inform their policies. They claimed that the busiest supervised consumption site in the country was embezzling money and shut it down. An RCMP investigation later found that not a single dollar was missing. The site was not reopened.

The report published by the government cited things like the increase in number of police calls around the Calgary supervised consumption site, conveniently leaving out the evidence that there was no actual increase in crime, just in concerned calls. Although the report provided a voice for a small handful of angry people, it also provided a reflection of our society.

You see, our society does not know how to be around people who are intoxicated, and this unknowning produces fear. We've lost the small-town feel where everyone knew to watch out for the drunk men stumbling home along cobblestone paths from the pub. This is partly because we have isolated ourselves from people with addiction, and partly because the drugs we're dealing with nowadays are a lot scarier when people are intoxicated.

Meth-induced psychosis is essentially a break with reality. It can be dangerous, as dangerous as any form of psychosis. And the general public has no idea what to do when they come across someone who is intoxicated with meth. Opioid intoxication can make it look like a person is sleeping or passed out—only they aren't breathing. People don't know what to do when they come across this. And alcohol intoxication can look belligerent, with shouting and breaking things. Again, people don't know what to do. This is how the police get involved. This discomfort feels like it should be criminal.

If, as a society, we want to be able to reduce addiction, we need to increase connection, to see a person who is intoxicated as a person. To learn the skills required to assess the safety of a situation. To know who to call for help if needed. To accept people who are intoxicated in our neighborhoods. You see, not all people who are intoxicated are dangerous. Learning who is and who isn't, learning what to do, and how to navigate it—all these are skills that our society has forgotten. But it can be taught. Just ask the many shelter staff who spend every day with people who are intoxicated. This is not an impossible skill. It just takes practice.

We also don't know how to be around people attempting abstinence. We glamorize drinking and drugs, and we hype movies that sensationalize substance use. Sober bars serving nonalcoholic drinks are lacking. We assume things about people with addiction that aren't true, forcing people to hide their struggle for sobriety for fear of judgment.

A couple of years ago I spoke at the Inhabit conference in Seattle run by the Parish Collective. The Parish Collective connects neighborhood churches to encourage one another in sharing stories of God at work. It was through preparing to share that I started being able to articulate the clear connection between the importance of neighborhood living in helping to heal addiction. Our society needs to not only provide outreach for patients, but to provide hospitality by opening up our yards, our neighborhoods, and our lives to make space for people with addiction. Whether intox or sober, people with addiction have an illness that requires us to adjust. We need to be brave, to be open, and to trust in a God who has made space for all people.

I was recently invited to participate in a rally to keep Calgary's supervised consumption site open.

"Who's running it?" I asked. We are a small community of addiction medicine practitioners, and nearly everyone knows everyone.

"Euan Thomson."

I had never heard of him. Suspicious, I asked around. We like to keep things local, and I didn't want some outsider using our struggle to pontificate on their own political soapbox for other things.

It turns out, I didn't know Euan because he wasn't in the field of addiction medicine. He ran a small business that met with clients near the supervised consumption site.

Euan had partnered up with other organizations to form EACH+EVERY: Businesses for Harm Reduction.

"EACH+EVERY: Businesses for Harm Reduction aims to reduce preventable drug poisoning deaths and help build a more fair and compassionate community by adding the voice of businesses to accelerate drug policy reform."[1]

Sick of the rhetoric of "protecting small businesses" being used as the reason the government was shutting down the SCS, EACH+EVERY was formed to raise the voice of businesses *in support* of people struggling with addiction.

---

1. https://www.eachandevery.org.

I was blown away. I assumed the rally was going to be a bunch of medical professionals and patients, all the same faces I knew, protesting the closure. I did not for a moment imagine that it would be small businesses taking the lead. One of the founding businesses, Annex Ale, produces my favorite nonalcoholic beverage. I had been hyping it up to all our friends just because it was really good. I didn't even realize that they were supporting my work. It was another merging of worlds, reminding me that God did not leave his presence only for my work life, but that he was present even in the taste of a really excellent ginger beer.

Little miracles like this have changed my perception of what is possible. I cannot even imagine what the world would be like if everyone had a good understanding of addiction medicine and a healthy dose of empathy and compassion. But I know that God has envisioned that world and is trying to help us get there. So all I can do is have faith, even if I can't see the end result.

The reality is, our world isn't divided, as much as sometimes I want it to be. My work life, my home life, my church life, and my neighborhood—these are all entwined. I'm someone who doesn't even like the different types of food to touch on my plate—at potlucks I go up with my plate several times because I can't just pile it all on. How will you taste each individual flavor otherwise? The thought of all my lives being actually mixed into one is a little stressful. But the reality is, I am trying to follow God in every sphere, and he unites all aspects of the world. So my neighborhood is not just about my home life.

I was in the middle of making dinner when I heard a knock at my door. I looked outside—there were two colleagues, a palliative care outreach nurse and a case manager. The case manager was crying. She smiled at me through her tears, "Can I sit on the deck for a debrief?" Of course, I nodded. It was peak COVID pandemic and she wasn't allowed inside by public health rules, but we could sit, distanced on the deck, outdoors.

"Thank you for letting me stay here a minute."

"Of course," I answered. "Can I get you tea?"

Bringing out her drink and a box of Kleenex, I heard snippets of the story—it was one I knew from having heard about it from others.

The nurse had gotten involved with this patient's case a few months ago. He had presented to the hospital with AIDS-defining illness, which meant that he had the HIV virus for a long enough time without treatment that it had progressed to the disease of AIDS.

Many people in North America live normal lives with the HIV virus—modern medication has made it that so little of the virus remains in the blood that it's undetectable. These people have almost no risk of illness or of transmitting HIV to others. Their primary battle is with stigma.

This patient, however, had a high viral load. He had been unable to organize the chaos of his life enough to make it to the one HIV clinic in all of southern Alberta. His addiction meant that the primary thing his brain could do was seek out more drugs. Time was a moving target. Making an appointment to see a physician, then getting blood work done regularly, picking up medications regularly from a pharmacy, getting taxes done so he could get medication coverage . . . the barriers were endless. He was so likely to stop taking his medications that he ran the risk of creating resistance in the virus. Starting and stopping an antiretroviral medication is a bit like starting and stopping an antibiotic. It gives the pathogen a chance to fight back, to mutate and develop resistance to that treatment which may no longer work. The risk was too high.

Instead, the focus for this patient became harm reduction. Teaching him about not sharing needles as he struggled with an addiction to opioids and to meth. Trying to limit the spread while building rapport, with the hopes that he would one day get to a place of greater stability, and would trust the healthcare system once he got there.

Unfortunately, before that could happen, this patient ended up in the hospital. He was unlikely to survive for much longer. They consulted the palliative care team, and the nurse got involved. He sat with the patient and had conversations about his goals at end of life. One thing was clear—he did not want to die in the hospital. The nurse brought this to the team, and he was moved to hospice.

In hospice, however, the healthcare team struggled. Used to caring for dying little old ladies in their eighties with doting sombre family members huddled around the deathbed, the staff did not know what to do with this patient. Using substances in the room, swearing at the top of his lungs, and disrupting the peace of the death of others—he was an outcast. The hospice that he was at was a for-profit facility. Soundproofing the rooms was not in the cards. He was kicked out of hospice.

What happens when a person is kicked out of a hospice? Well, it means they return to their former life on the street. Patients dying in shelter on a mat, or outside on a riverbank, freezing in a tent or huddling by a building vent—this is how patients die who have palliative illnesses and are homeless. They may be dying of cancer, or of infection, or heart disease—anything that someone without an addiction might die of. But the end looks different, often because of addiction.

The palliative care team worked hard to try to find alternatives for this patient. Finally, a harm-reduction housing building had a space open up. The team knew the staff well, and they were a good fit. The patient moved in. The staff there, despite having little to no healthcare training, and being paid slightly over minimum wage, had the skill set to handle his behaviors. He was able to see people he knew and was not left alone unless he wanted it. Home care nursing came in to help him sometimes, but it was often a different nurse every time. He didn't know them and often refused care. This nurse had just been called in the day before because the patient had soiled himself and was refusing anyone entry to the room. Shame and anger had compounded in his delirium, and he would not allow help. But when a familiar face entered the room, he accepted. Soon, the nurse had the patient cleaned up, bathed, and tucked in for the night.

It was the next day that the case manager got called in after hours. The patient died in bed, with the building staff present, looking at them as he went. The staff even had the presence of mind to be playing his favorite music. It was a good death, with a roof over his head, tucked into bed, and with people there who cared about him. Still, the grief of such a preventable loss overwhelmed all the staff who had loved this patient in his final days. He was the case manager's first palliative patient. She had loved him deeply, cared for him, taken him to the bank and argued with him that he should not tell her his PIN number. She helped him regain some semblance of a normal life. She witnessed the barriers he faced, the injustice he experienced. Her heart broke when he died.

So they came over after he died, to have a safe space to grieve. She ate a box of grief donuts while pouring her heart into the box of tissues beside her. The tears flowed freely as she recounted stories of her patient.

Darkness fell, and it was time to go. They got up to leave, stuffing used tissues into their pockets so I wouldn't have to clean them up after them. "Thanks so much for having us over. It's really lucky that you live so close."

That's when I realized. The building that I was so nervous about—the PSH one that moved in a few blocks away—that was the building that had offered space to this dying man. Those were the staff who loved him. Living so close meant that I could be available quickly to support everyone involved. It meant that the nurse and case manager could debrief in the warmth of a home space rather than quickly by the cars. This man who had just died was my neighbor.

Throughout Scripture, it is evident that geography matters—it is a theme woven through every story, and through several parables. The place where people live is often featured in the story as a critical part to understanding who those people are. Where we live is a part of who we are. The actual land matters in the story. Loving our neighbors means paying attention to our geographical neighborhoods. You can't choose your neighbors, just like you can't choose who sits in the pew near you in church. Loving your neighbors is a different thing than loving your friends, or your family, or your colleagues. It means welcoming people whatever their struggles may be, simply because they live near you. We know that addiction is part of every neighborhood—overdose rates are high in the suburbs, where people use drugs secretly for fear that the neighbors will see. People put themselves at risk of death with nobody there to help them if they overdose, because of fear of being seen in their shame. In your own neighborhood, can you see addiction? How can you join God in his love for people who are addicted in your community? These are questions I would love to see asked in each church, in each Christian home, and in the heart of each individual Jesus-follower.

I'm part of a community neighborhood watch Facebook page that many in my neighborhood have joined. People report crimes that have happened to them, and talk about things they're doing to protect their property. It can be really helpful. A few weeks ago, a kid in the neighborhood went missing, and the Facebook pages blew up with posts. Everyone left their house, searching for the kid, posting if they'd heard anything, communicating which areas of the community they had already checked. He was found safe a few hours later, thanks in part to a neighborhood that came together.

But sometimes on the neighborhood watch page people post descriptions of people caught on cameras stealing packages, and warn everyone to watch out for them. People get classified into criminals, often without much proof. Members of the page are encouraged to "keep an eye out" for shifty characters.

To me, this creates an atmosphere of fear. When we look out our windows and see someone we don't recognize, we immediately narrow our eyes and wonder if they are there to harm us or take our things. If they behave erratically, or walk while stumbling, our fears are confirmed. They are dangerous. They must be watched.

We don't notice the moment we became the vigilantes of the neighborhood, suspicious and reacting to our fears. We believe that the person's addiction, skin color, age, or whatever other reason, puts them at fault for causing our anxiety. We can't see their humanity; we only see whether or not they pose a threat. Courage is channelled exclusively into protection rather than hospitality.

My neighbor across the street, Anna, watches out her window a lot. She knows every time I go into the yard, and she knows everyone who walks down the street. She also knows where the birds have nested in my big spruce tree, and she knows when my cats are in the window. She notices everything. And she does so with a smile and a wave. Anna is four, and she spends a lot of her time watching the television that is her front window. When I wave, I always receive frantic waves back. She looks into her neighborhood with eager interest, observing without judging, trying to learn.

What would happen if we learned from Anna? What if we approached the world with curiosity and joy?

As Christians, what if we sought to honor God's image in each human living near us?

I honestly believe that this is the primary way to solve the opioid crisis. It starts right in our own neighborhoods and extends through our love into the people near us, into our healthcare systems, our voting patterns, our laws, and thus into the deepest morals of our society. Change starts on your own street.

10

Free Will

BABY JAIL. IT WAS the only way.

Every time the door was accidentally left unlocked on the house across the street, the little boy would sprint across the road to my house. I'd find him in various states of disarray—once naked and soapy, giggling in my yard—inevitably being pursued by a frantic parent. He had developmental delays and had a hard time remembering rules. But he knew what he wanted, and the impulse to come over and hang out among the sunflowers was strong. As soon as his siblings provided a distraction, he was up and moving.

The problem was the road. It wasn't a busy road, but it was at a spot where cars turned. Nobody expected a soapy naked kid to sprint into the street at that spot, unless you lived there. The danger was terrifying for us adults.

We tried everything to make my yard less appealing to him. I put up a gate, but that just meant he spent longer on the street trying to get the gate open. I cut down the sunflowers, but he liked the grass anyway. I pointed out the grass that was truly much greener on his side of the street, but he didn't care. He wanted to be in the yard across the street.

So, baby jail. Anytime the door was to be opened, groceries were to be carried in, or yard work was to be done, he was put in baby jail. Essentially it was a set of barriers in a corner of the room that he couldn't overcome. It wasn't isolation because he could see and interact with everyone. He just couldn't get out.

Yes, it was demeaning, but it was to protect him. Dignity was not a consideration. His parents just didn't know what else to do. It only lasted about six months, and then he outgrew the appeal of my yard. We all breathed a sigh of relief, and the baby jail was retired. It had kept him alive.

That same concept of keeping someone trapped until they are safe is sometimes applied in medicine. Under the Province of Alberta's Mental Health Act, when someone is in an acute state of mental illness in which they might pose an imminent harm to themselves or others, they can be forced by a physician or a police officer to go to a hospital for medical assessment. This certification lasts twenty-four hours. Once they are assessed in a hospital, if they are deemed to be a continued risk to themselves or others, psychiatry can fill out a different form to keep them certified until the patient is no longer so severely unwell.

This form does not allow for forced treatment, only for a forced stay in the hospital. The patient also has access to a review panel, which looks at several key items when deciding whether or not to cancel a patient's certifications. It looks to see if the patient's stay in the hospital is actually beneficial. It looks to see if the patient has enough autonomy to choose for themselves if they want to leave the hospital. And it looks to see if there is risk to others if the patient leaves.

The complexities of the Mental Health Act are sometimes cumbersome, but they are necessary. There is a loss of dignity that comes with a loss of autonomy. God gave every human free will, and it is a serious thing to take away something that God gave. We only do this when we absolutely have to.

We all are given the choice to do things that are bad for us, that might kill us. We do not certify people for eating cheeseburgers after a heart attack, or for skiing in avalanche terrain, or for drinking soda pop when they have diabetes. So the criteria for certification are intentionally demanding. They force us to seriously consider the importance of personal freedom. They also force us to be realistic about whether or not removing a person's freedoms will actually help them.

This is the key difference between the criminal system and the healthcare system when it comes to locking somebody up. In healthcare, we cannot justify holding a patient if by doing so we are not helping them—or, worse, we are causing harm.

A few weeks ago, I had a patient appointment in my clinic schedule. I was pleasantly surprised, since it was for a patient I knew was living on the streets, using fentanyl and meth. He had survived several overdoses in the past few months that had left him barely clinging to life in the ICU. It was a miracle he was still alive. I felt helpless in caring for him, since this was a patient who was not able to maintain treatment and consistently declined help. I was surprised that the patient had called and booked an appointment.

I walked into the room and suddenly realized what had happened. A familiar-looking man sat in the chair. He looked up when I came in, and I was struck by his gaze. It was the same gaze I knew from my patient, but something was different. He wore an expensive Arc'teryx jacket and Blundstone boots, and his hair was done. It took a second to click.

"Hi, I'm Eric*. I'm Philip's* brother."

I explained that I could not give out any information about Philip's care without Philip present.

"I know. He couldn't make it in. I just wanted to see if there's anything I can do to get him into treatment."

Eric poured his heart out. I sat and listened, not allowed to say anything about his brother, as he talked about the abuse his little brother had experienced at the hands of a hockey coach. Their paths diverged as Philip's unprocessed trauma led him to numb the pain with substances. While Eric had become a lawyer, Philip had become a homeless man. But their childhood bond remained.

Eric had learned how to have boundaries, how to show love without going broke, and was himself in counseling. He knew how to care for himself and still love his brother. But he had heard about something called "involuntary treatment" and he wanted to know more.

"If there is any chance at all that by forcing Philip into treatment I could save his life, I'll do it."

I could see the pain and the love etched into the worry lines on Eric's face. Involuntary treatment was not being suggested punitively, or just as a way to clean up the streets. It was being suggested out of desperation and love.

"Philip is not himself. You didn't know the real Philip. Who he is now—that's not who he was. The drugs have taken over."

Eric's words had truth to them. People who use substances are usually not the same person they were when they were sober. Often, people who have been able to maintain abstinence look back on the person they were when using, and they hate that version of themselves. They long to distance their new selves from that person, out of shame and fear. There is no doubt that a person with a substance use disorder is no longer the same person as they used to be.

To say this is not, however, the same thing as claiming that such a person has no grasp on reality, lost in active psychosis. Having a substance use disorder does not justify certification under the mental health act because people who use substances still have a sense of reality, and they particularly understand right and wrong. They may be a different person than they used to be, but they are allowed to be who they are.

People who use substances are worthy of love, even while they are in active use. They have dignity and their autonomy must be respected. I am always wary when people in recovery talk about their prior substance-using selves with disrespect. Recovery progresses when people are able to look back on who they were with compassion, and to show love to their earlier selves as an integral part of who they have become.

Eric loved Philip as he was now, despite his longing for the brother he remembered—and dreamed of. There is a deep grief that comes with understanding that someone we love is not who we hoped they would be. When we see loved ones following paths that we would not choose, that we cannot follow, it is heartwrenching. Watching them hurt themselves, or hurt others, and feeling helpless, creates a pain that reverberates through every part of your body. It makes complete sense to try to control our loved ones, to keep them safe, out of love.

We have to remember that this is the same pain that God feels as he watches us, his children, hurt one another. There are dissertations, textbooks, and multitudes of sermons all with the theme of "Why God allows wrongdoing in the world." Theologians have debated this concept over the ages. Humans have struggled with faith that God is good in a world in which people are allowed to cause such harm. I am not a theologian and I don't feel confident giving a clear theological answer to why God allows this.

What I do know is that he does allow it. He chooses to allow each of us our own free will. I can only imagine the pain that he feels when we make poor choices, and particularly when we harm one another. I think that this same pain is reflected in the pain of the family members of people who struggle with substance use disorders.

The pain of watching his brother suffer led to Eric's desperation in trying to have Philip forced into treatment. Eric wanted Philip to live, to get better, and ultimately to become the brother he remembered. Eric was willing to look past the ethics of removing Philip's autonomy if it would save his life.

But would it save his life?

The scientific evidence around involuntary treatment is mixed at best. People forced into treatment are, by some studies, twice as likely to die by overdose after being released. People who access treatment voluntarily have significant benefits from treatment that are not reflected in studies of people who access treatment involuntarily.

The issue is not only that treatment is not effective. It is that when people are forced, they are at higher risk of death afterwards. And this makes sense. We cannot treat a disease that reduces people's ability to choose by removing the rest of their ability to choose. The goal of treatment is to increase the autonomy of people. It requires invitation, not coercion.

When we reduce the options available to patients, we force family members into feeling they must choose involuntary treatment for their loved one. Instead, we should be providing housing, wrap-around supports, case management, and voluntary treatment, all of which have been shown to be much more effective—and *cost*-effective—as a solution. The current scandal is that these resources are so limited.

In Calgary, the wait time to get into treatment can be several months. The wait-list for housing is often much longer. People find themselves learning how to winterize their *tents* in order to avoid sleeping in overcrowded shelters in the winters—and these are winters that can see forty below zero. (Forty below is where the Celsius and Fahrenheit scales meet. Forty below is forty below, and it's terrifyingly cold.) Paradoxically, hospital admissions for frostbite *and burns* both spike through the winter—with the burns coming from people trying to heat their outdoor shelters. Funding involuntary treatment instead of housing and a universal basic income, both interventions that have shown to reduce substance use disorders, simply does not make sense. Forcing some people into treatment when other people are lining up outside of detoxes, begging for a spot—this does not make sense.

When we shift from invitation into coercion, we inevitably require leverage. For someone who has almost nothing left, there isn't much we can threaten to take away. This could be their housing (you are required to complete treatment in order to access housing). Another way to phrase that is to say, "You do not deserve housing unless you have gone to treatment."

It could also be their freedom ("Go into treatment or we'll put you in jail"), which is problematic if there is no other reason for them to be imprisoned.

We are telling people they do not deserve their freedom because they use substances. This is a very different paradigm than the paradigm of drug court, which has good evidence to show it is effective. Drug court says, "You have committed this criminal act [such as stealing] because of your substance use disorder. Instead of jail, you can access treatment." It says, "According to our laws, you deserve jail. But we will offer you healthcare instead because we understand that treatment will be more effective than jail." *Treatment is more effective than jail.* Nobody should be surprised by this. We can't say for sure, however, that treatment is more effective than housing, or than basic income, and so we cannot refuse these things coercively until a patient goes to treatment.

Denying people freedom, housing, or healthcare in order to enforce involuntary treatment, an intervention that has not been shown to be effective and carries twice the risk of death, is simply wrong. Again, this should come as no surprise to Christians. God chooses not to deny us our free will, no matter what paths we find ourselves on. He sets the standard for how we are to treat one another. It is hard to resist the temptation to coerce loved ones toward a healthier path, but we must resist it. We may badly wish things were different than they are, but this is how it is. And this is how it must be.

11

Judgment

A FEW YEARS AGO, I was on a walk with a friend of mine from church, Teresa*. We lived near each other, and it was nice to walk through the streets and pray for our neighborhood. These prayer walks helped us become aware of the goings-on outside our own circles, and sometimes provided opportunities for us to meet new friends.

On one of these walks, Teresa pointed out a little house with fading ceramic statuary decorating the front walk. It was a bit shabby, but had the most beautiful flowers in the yard. If I had to guess, I'd say an older gardener lived there, one who didn't have the ability to patch the shingles but still tried to care for the flowers. There are many homes like this in our neighborhood, and most have the original owners still living there.

"I'm pretty sure that hedge is too high for bylaw." I hadn't noticed that the hedge that ran between this house and the next one was quite tall.

"How do you know?" I asked.

"It's supposed to be no taller than 6 feet. I think that's probably 6.5, maybe even 7 feet."

On closer inspection, it looked like the sides of the hedge had been trimmed, but they couldn't reach the top of the hedge.

JUDGMENT

"I wonder if they need help," I mused. A guy on my street ran a landscaping business and gave significant discounts to neighbors and people who are elderly—sometimes working for free. Making these neighborly connections was part of the fun of investing in a neighborhood. I looked over. Teresa was looking through her contacts on her phone. I saw her pull up "bylaw."

"You have bylaw as one of your contacts?"

"Yeah," she replied. "The hedge is too high. This should be reported."

"Wait—don't you think we should talk to them before just calling bylaw? They could get a ticket! Maybe they need help!" I was appalled.

She stared at me, equally appalled. "Talk to them? We don't know them!"

In her mind, the responsibility of all people was to follow the law at all times. Her responsibility was to make sure the law was enforced when she perceived that it was being broken. This was how she understood justice.

But this view failed to take into account the rest of the story. It skipped right over structural injustice. Gentrification of our neighborhood had driven house prices up, to the point that some of the older people on our street had trouble paying property taxes on homes they'd owned their whole lives. The exorbitant cost of private long-term care facilities combined with the long wait for public spots meant that many people ended up staying in their homes for longer than they should have. And lots of seniors in our neighborhood had very low incomes, barely enough to get by on. Calling bylaw because a senior couldn't cut their hedge, giving them a ticket they'd have to starve to pay—was this justice? We didn't know the owner's story. Maybe it was a wealthy mogul who was not investing in the neighborhood and needed to be held accountable. But maybe it was a low-income senior who needed someone to notice they were struggling and provide comfort. Without presence, we couldn't be sure.

This story, to me, highlights some of the ways that the church has failed to understand their role in the world. By choosing to follow Jesus, we have committed to seeking a deeper understanding of what is sacred—where every human is made in the image of God, we all recognize the sin within us, and we accept the grace given to us by a God who loves us sacrificially. This invitation from God inspires us to think lovingly and creatively about our responses to injustices so that when someone steals a coat from us, we give them the rest of the clothes we have too. If someone hits us on one cheek, we turn the other and let them hit that one as well. It rails against the perceived notions of justice that society has set up, and forces us to understand that grace is the only way forward. Following Jesus does not always mean following the laws of the world. In fact, several people who followed Jesus ended up in prison because of it. Being able to enter a scenario and ask what Jesus would do reminds me of the cheesy "WWJD" bracelets that people used to wear. But the mnemonic is not wrong. Being able to stop and ask, "Where is God in this situation? How can I join in his work?" is the whole point of being a Christian.

"She shouldn't be doing that," the nurse snarled at me, as I gowned up in front of a patient room in the hospital. Julie* was on isolation due to pneumonia, and I needed to wear a gown, mask, gloves, and eye protection before heading in. It took a while to put it all on.

"I'm sorry, what?"

"Your patient. You people keep telling her it's okay to use drugs. She shouldn't be doing that."

So many misconceptions all in one seething rant. I looked at the nurse, surprised. She was nearly bent double, finger wagging in my face, red faced, with a beautiful ombre floral scrub top. A little silver cross dangled from her neck, burning pain into my heart. Julie could hear her through the open door.

"She's a liar! She obviously doesn't want help. She keeps using drugs and then denying it. I know she's lying. She should be discharged. Get her out of this hospital."

JUDGMENT

"I'm not lying! And I'm not a bad person!" Julie yelled this, then started crying in her room, unable to come out to face her accuser because of isolation restrictions.

As calmly as I could, I mustered, "This is an inappropriate conversation. You need to take a minute. I am going in to speak with the patient. I can address your concerns after." I entered the room and shut the door, fingers tingling with adrenaline, face a mask of calm.

Inside the room, Julie sobbed. "She keeps calling me a liar! I'm not using!"

Choosing to avoid pointing out the used foils, burnt spoon, and baggies littering her bedside table, I sat down on the chair beside the bed.

"Hi, my name is Dr. Meera. I'm one of the addiction doctors at this hospital. My job is to support you in helping you reach your goals around substance use. I'm very sorry that nurse shouted at you. It was out of line."

Julie hiccuped herself into silence and looked at me. "I swear I'm not using."

"To me, you using isn't the biggest thing. I want you to be able to stay and get treatment for your pneumonia. No point in talking about using if you're dead from a lung infection."

She cracked a smile. Dark humor was something she understood.

"That nurse won't give me any of my pain medications. She says I'm addicted to them."

A common problem. In the age of fentanyl, there is just nothing as good as a street supply anymore. Patients don't come to hospitals seeking drugs because the street drugs are much cheaper, much easier to access, and much more potent than anything we prescribe in the hospital. But these perceptions linger among healthcare staff.

"I know. The pain meds are probably barely touching your pain." Julie looked at me in astonishment, surprised that I would have this view.

I sighed and started explaining the science of fentanyl. Fentanyl is more potent than the hydromorphone she was on in the hospital. The illicit stuff she had been using was exponentially higher in dose than what she was prescribed. So on top of having constant pain, she was feeling stigmatized for being drug-seeking. She felt trapped, like there was no way to succeed. And she wanted to leave the hospital.

"Can you explain that to the nurse?"

"I'll try," I said.

"I'll try to stop using, too," Julie said. "Please don't kick me out. I don't want to die."

Building rapport with her was about meeting her where she was at. If I had challenged her at the beginning when she said she wasn't using, it would have led to an antagonistic relationship rather than a therapeutic one. It wasn't about being right. It was about maintaining relationship.

After leaving the room, the nurse was nowhere to be found. "I'll just put in an order to increase the dose," I thought to myself, keen to avoid confrontation. The nurse couldn't disobey the direct order, and Julie would be okay. I walked out of the unit, hoping to not notice the nurse. Halfway down the hallway to my next patient, I stopped. I could hear God calling me back. Trying to ignore him, I rationalized like crazy. "I am a doctor in a hospital in a pandemic! I do not have time to babysit that nurse." But the still small voice kept at me. God is one heck of a persistent fella.

I turned around. I couldn't find the nurse so I asked the receptionist to find the charge nurse for me. "She's in a meeting." I nodded, grateful at the excuse to leave. But the still small voice kept going. "Can you interrupt it for a minute?" I asked, resignedly. Turns out the meeting was with the bedside nurse for Julie, who was complaining to the charge nurse that we needed to discharge the patient. They invited me into the room and the charge nurse turned toward me and asked what they should do.

"Before we get started, I would like to say that I felt your behavior toward me, shouting at me in the hallway in front of the patient, was highly unprofessional and concerning." It just came out. I didn't mean to blame, but to hold accountable. The nurse deflated. She took a second, with both myself and the charge nurse looking at her.

"I'm sorry. I got carried away."

I was blown away at her willingness to be called on it. "Thank you for your apology."

The charge nurse explained that this nurse was very passionate about staff safety, having been part of an incident where a staff member was hurt previously. That passion was good, but it was being taken a little bit out of context with this patient. We talked about the patient, strategies to manage use in the hospital when there was no supervised consumption site on site, and how to build rapport with Julie. I was able to focus on how to keep staff safe while also maintaining relationship with the patient. I told her about Julie's history of trauma, about my approach with Julie, and gave the nurse tips on how to rebuild trust.

Later that afternoon, I took a look at Julie's chart. There was a note from the nurse. "Earlier today, the writer was angry at the patient for suspected use and shouted at the patient and the doctor who was there. Writer spoke with the doctor and learned about addiction. Writer went back to the patient room and apologized. The patient accepted writer's apology. Writer had a long conversation with patient, who was very kind to writer and who shared her story. Will continue to build rapport."

I couldn't believe she had written that in Julie's charting. I had never seen documentation like that before. That level of integrity—it suddenly struck me. This nurse was actually serious about what it meant to follow Jesus. She lost her way in the moment, but she found it again through restored relationship. That still small voice that called me back—it wasn't to help Julie. It was to help the nurse.

Julie continued to use illicit drugs while in the hospital until we could get the dosage of her pain medication right. She eventually started on treatment for her opioid use disorder. By the time she was discharged, she was looking a lot better. And she had built a friendship with this nurse. They saw a shared humanity in one another.

I feel like a huge part of my job is advocating that people approach my patients with kindness and grace, meeting them where they are at. But the reality is, God doesn't only love my patients. He loves everyone. This means my job involves meeting everyone where they are at. It means loving the sticklers of the world, not cancelling them. It means extending kindness even when I feel there is injustice at work. It means that when a doctor is rude to my patients, I need to learn how to approach them with kindness instead of channelling my bent for justice into a rage. Because the reality is, the problems with drugs in our society aren't solely because of people who use drugs. We all bear the guilt of how our society has failed to keep people healthy. It would take a miracle to fix some of these problems. Luckily, I believe in miracles.

12

Personal Change

THOUGHTS AND PRAYERS. How did this phrase of compassion and faith become such a symbol for inaction in the world?

This Christian phrase pops up every time people want to make fun of the lack of interest from the world about a serious topic.

"The world is burning."

"Well, thoughts and prayers! I need a latte."

When we hear about difficult topics, a natural response is to distance oneself. It's just that this isn't meant to be the Christian response. It isn't meant to be the healthcare response.

Thoughts and prayers are still where I think we should start. Just a bit more genuinely. Here is my tried and true three step process toward acting on the information you've learned.

STEP 1. LOOK INWARD

Allowing your eyes and your mind to roam into the lives of people who struggle with addiction—noticing them—is the first step toward caring for them. Spending time thinking about your own personal complicity, regardless of your faith background or your healthcare knowledge—this is how we start. We start by looking at the logs in our own eyes.

So many factors have contributed to each of our personal beliefs about addiction. Maybe someone you loved has taken advantage of you, burned the relationship down, and left. It's always different when it's your family, and hopefully this book can broaden your perspective beyond the hurt that loved ones can cause. Maybe you learned about drugs in school and firmly believed that only bad people take them. Maybe you believed that being a good Christian means following all laws. Maybe you are in recovery, and you have achieved sobriety without medications and without therapy. All these are legitimate experiences with legitimate consequences. But just like any one book of Scripture, they are incomplete without the rest of the stories. And there are many, many stories of God working among people who have addictions in the world. No one story can define the way he works. I have written about several of my experiences in this book, but to be honest, each day of work has as many new stories as there are patients. The beautiful thing about this is that hope pops up in unexpected ways. The mystery of God means that you just don't know for sure where he might show up—you've gotta keep looking around.

Of course I don't mean giving up all boundaries and showing up to shelters naively. I mean doing the internal work to learn how to love people with addictions well, in ways that honor all involved. Actually one of my favorite books is *Boundaries* by Dr. Henry Cloud and Dr. John Townsend—I have bought several copies and never seem to have any on my shelf because I am constantly giving them out. There is no healthy way to love people without boundaries.

I have been practicing remembering to be happy when I find out I'm being offensive. It means that the world has improved much faster than I have improved, and it is an opportunity to catch up.

"We don't say 'retarded,' it's offensive because it implies people with disabilities are somehow lesser, behind."

When I hear things like this, I don't think, "I can't say anything anymore!" I think, "Wow, I hadn't thought of that. Of course that would be offensive. I need to be more careful with my words and not just accept the language of my youth. I'm glad I was corrected."

There is a joy in learning to love better that I think we are missing as a society. That joy is also inherent to being Christian. We all know that none of us is perfect, and yet we all strive to do better. Learning to love with our words is part of this.

Did anything in this book stand out to you? Were you convicted? Sit with the discomfort. Part of the work of assessing situations fairly is to acknowledge personal bias.

I was an interviewer for a medical school a couple of years ago. In the pre-interview training, we were taught that simple things such as holding a hot drink instead of a cold one, skewed interviewers' perceptions of the candidates. So many factors influence our decisions. The key to fairness is becoming aware of these factors. All of us interviewers were prejudiced somehow. The key was looking into the mirror and sitting with the discomfort. Once able to do this, we were able to name the prejudice, bring the darkness into the light and dispel it.

The first step toward helping people with addiction is to name the beliefs you have had that are wrong. Say them out loud. Dispel them.

Therapy helped me learn how to change my mind. It helped me become closer to who I want to be—to let go of the painful things in my past instead of holding them tight and seeking validation. It helped me to be more objective with my own patients, so when patients reminded me of people I didn't like, I didn't take it out on them. If you are struggling with letting go of some of your preconceived notions, even though deep down you know they may not be true, seek help. This is a human thing to do. I personally believe that everyone should be in therapy, the way I believe everyone should see a family doctor regularly, whether they are sick or not. It is basic preventative medicine.

So be open to changing your mind and to seeking the truth about yourself and your own relationship with the Creator.

STEP 2. LOOK UP

My med school university's motto is "Mo Shule Togam Suas," or "I will lift up mine eyes." It comes from Psalm 121:1, "I will lift up mine eyes unto the hills, from whence cometh my help?" The psalm refers to looking to God. The university means it's looking to education. I think both of these can be true.

Science is the pursuit of truth about the world. Theology is the pursuit of truth about God. Both of these are needed if the Christian approach to addiction is to reflect God's presence among the afflicted.

To the Christians reading this, I say this: you must start with education about theology. Take a course on the New Testament's interpretation of the Old. See how Jesus interpreted the laws he was born into, and how he approached the religious beliefs that drove people away from God. Learn how to love by learning how God loved people through the ages. Commit to lifelong learning about God and keep a posture of seeking him. Pray. And as you continue to learn and grow in relationship with God, apply his teachings to the world around you, including figuring out how to love people with addiction.

To all reading this, I say this: you must arm yourself with education about addiction. If you're in healthcare, do the free online trainings about opioid use disorder. Shadow your addiction medicine colleagues. Everyone should go to an educational site hosted on a reserve near you and ask questions about Indigenous ways of knowing in your area. And most importantly, listen to people who use drugs. Not just people who have succeeded at abstinence—get to know people who are actively using as well. Invite shelter staff to teach you skills or conduct workshops around how to safely interact with people who are intoxicated. The War on Drugs has turned into a war on people who use drugs. Make a conscious decision to end the war, and show up on the side of those who have suffered.

PERSONAL CHANGE

STEP 3. CHOOSE TO ACT

Just as Jesus asked the rich young ruler to give up all that he clung to, you too are required to give up your comfort. Whether this be money, or certainty, or time, you are asked to step away from it. Only you will know what Jesus asks of you. Be willing to follow.

Spending time in the presence of people who have addictions can be uncomfortable. Addiction can lead to poverty, which can lead to shelters with bad smells, lengthy hacking coughs, and dirty feet. Presence in these spaces means looking past these smells, to seeing human beings. It also means learning new languages—learning how people use curse words, what they mean, and what street slang is. Calling someone "a goof" in the streets of Calgary is liable to get someone killed—this term refers in street slang to a pedophile, and it is the most offensive word on the streets. When we have such distinct subcultures in one city that we don't speak each others' languages, there is a problem. When a person who is addicted shows up in the hospital and yells "Fuck!" loudly when getting an IV, all the nurses glare. But maybe they're just speaking a different language. Maybe that word in their language means, "I'm scared and in pain." Learn the meaning behind the language.

There is also discomfort in facing the stigma that we may have unknowingly perpetuated. I look back at the article that kicked off my advocacy work and realize that I used a very stigmatizing term in the title—"addict." It is a term that defines a person by their illness, which is against everything I am trying to do. We don't use terms like that in the field anymore, although back then it was common. Now, person-centered language is expected in professional circles. I cringe every time the article comes up, because it's so stigmatizing. Still, all I can do is learn from my mistakes and move forward. I am constantly trying to improve my own language skills by learning from the people I hurt. I try to use the term "died by suicide" instead of "committed suicide," to avoid criminalizing such a painful situation. When patients who are transgender present with different pronouns, I have to catch myself and make sure I use the preferred pronouns that will cause the patient the least harm. Language matters, and even if it means I have to pause, try to remember the correct term, and then continue, it matters that I keep trying.

Being present in difficult situations also means advocacy. It means at family dinners, when someone tells a story about a drunk guy weaving between cars panhandling, you speak up and reduce the stigma. I personally have a really hard time with this—I see red every time someone says, "So what? Let them die. They chose this." But these comments stem from ignorance. Getting uncomfortable can look like stepping into those spaces of ignorance, and refuting them. It means not tolerating hate speech, racist comments, or dehumanizing terms.

If the thing you are convicted to do is to share the money you're stewarding, then find places to give that aren't already basking in the wealth of the majority of Christians in your city. Many Christian organizations have more money than the secular ones because of donations from churches. This leads to resentment against Christian agencies. Instead, give to the agencies that are willing to help keep those actively addicted alive. Give to political parties whose policies follow science and who are willing to embrace terms like harm reduction. Give your votes to those parties too. Give to lawyers who are giving up paid cases to help fight for justice.

These three steps, when followed with an open mind and a prayerful heart, will lead you to a path that helps people with addiction. I believe that it will also help you become closer to the Creator.

13

Structural Change

I HAD BEEN WORRYING for days about how to break the news to my patient. We both knew the implications: she was likely to relapse. But there was no other option. We had tried everything else.

A few days earlier, we had received word from the government. "Safer supply," or the prescribing of medications that were safer than those headlining the illicit toxic drug crisis, had been made illegal in our province. We were expected to transition all our safer supply patients to specific long-acting opioid agonist therapies (OAT), and we had a very short time in which to do so. The problem was, this patient had already tried OAT unsuccessfully. Safer supply was never, for me, a first-line therapy. It was reserved for a small handful of my patients under very demanding criteria.

Rosaline was one of those patients. A year earlier, when we first met, she was keen to get off of illicit fentanyl. After becoming a paraplegic, she had developed an opioid use disorder, and slowly lost everything in her life. She was often found in shelters, without a wheelchair, crawling around using her arms. Her legs dragged behind her, covered in sores. Her motivation to finally make a change was the loss of her partner in an overdose. Rosaline was determined to become a peer-support staff member, and her goal was to start working for the health system.

Why I Help People Take Drugs

I tried her on Suboxone, but her blood pressure could not tolerate it. She tried methadone and Kadian both, but neither were effective for her. Finally, when we conducted a trial of replacement hydromorphone, she was able to come off the fentanyl. Regular urine drug screens combined with an honest personality showed that we were successful. She was housed, and she kept her new electric wheelchair without it getting stolen. She was doing well.

Suddenly, the new legislation came into effect. I was no longer allowed to prescribe her hydromorphone. If she had chronic pain, I could have continued it—but because of her paraplegia, the sores on her legs actually didn't hurt. I had no choice. I risked losing my own license to continue to prescribe it to her. I had to break the news.

Rosaline did not want me to lose my license. She couldn't understand why this new legislation had come into play, or what it had to do with her. It was hard for her to comprehend that I was effectively "cutting her off." Of course, I replaced the hydromorphone with OAT, in an effort to keep her out of withdrawal. But it was not effective. Within a month after stopping the hydromorphone, she had lost her housing and her wheelchair. Two weeks later, her name showed up in my daily mail from the medical examiner's office. She had overdosed and died.

In the making of public policy, the voices of patients and of front-line staff must be heard alongside those of scientific research into effective interventions. Too often, well-intentioned policies cause harm because their implications are not well understood by policymakers. Politicians, claiming to be led by what they enjoy calling "common sense," frequently fail to understand that complex problems sometimes require complex solutions. Legislating blanket bans has consequences that patients and physicians could readily predict, but policymakers may not be able to.

I hope that the stories in this book have helped you to understand that the practice of caring effectively and compassionately for people with addiction is not always intuitive, not always what a layperson might expect. Proper care is critically important to maintaining human dignity in our society and to reaching as many people as possible as effectively as possible with the best available treatment. But that treatment frequently isn't what the average person would expect it to be.

My own mind has changed repeatedly over my fifteen years of experience in this field, and I hope to keep allowing it to change as I continue to learn. As my own practices improve, the effects reach my patients and my prescriber community. I don't work in public policy, so anything I decide has somewhat limited effects. When we decide things for a society—via laws, criminalization, health policy—we produce outcomes that are much wider in reach. We have to treat this public implication with respect, even sacredness. Our public health doctors are the ones with the most education in how to do this well. So what do they say?

Public health research consistently supports the measures that I have endorsed in this book. In 2019, Dr. Bonnie Henry, the provincial health officer for British Columbia, wrote a special report, "Stopping the Harm: Decriminalization of People Who Use Drugs in BC."

> As BC's Provincial Health Officer, I have called on the federal government to move toward regulating access to currently controlled drugs, with a focus on harm reduction associated with the use of those substances, as well as the harms associated with the current prohibition-based regulatory regime and its application.
>
> But in the context of the continuing overdose crisis that is affecting families and communities across BC, the province cannot wait for action at the federal level. *Immediate provincial action is warranted, and I recommend that the Province of BC urgently move to decriminalize people who possess controlled substances for personal use.* This is an important additional step to stem the tide of unprecedented deaths.[1]

Before I started in this field, I might have written off Dr. Henry's words as the rant of a left-wing hippie who wants everyone to use drugs. Now I know better. She is one of the best-educated

---

1. Henry, "Stopping the Harm," 5; emphasis original.

professionals on this subject that Canada has produced. And there is a growing body of doctors—including public health physicians, addiction medicine specialists, emergency room doctors, and psychiatrists—who all say the same thing. What needs to change with our opioid crisis is not simply the patients. What needs to change is our society's posture toward people who use drugs.

A grim surprise lies in the dark statistics on the current opioid pandemic. Over half the people dying in this crisis don't actually have an addiction to opioids. They might have an addiction to alcohol or stimulant drugs, and they might use opioids recreationally—*without being addicted*. Their cause of death was not opioid addiction. It was contaminated supply. Once more, the situation is more complex than many people, including policymakers, understand.

I recognize that my ability and opportunity to treat the patients in front of me represents a massively inadequate drop in the bucket when tackling the opioid crisis. The problem must be dealt with at the level of public health. Public health doctors are the ones who taught us years ago that prohibition was ineffective, and they advocated instead for a safe and legal supply of alcohol. Public health doctors are now the ones leading the advocacy for a safe and legal supply of drugs in Canada. I truly believe they are doing God's work in the world.

And there is need for this work to be done worldwide. Although fentanyl is currently more of a North American concern, addiction is a global illness.

On June 23, 2023, the United Nations Human Rights Council published a statement by their special rapporteurs: "The 'war on drugs' may be understood to a significant extent as a war on people. . . . In various countries, the 'war on drugs' has been more effective as a system of racial control than as a tool to reduce drug markets. . . . Everyone without exception has the right to life-saving harm reduction interventions. . . . Criminalisation results in significant barriers to access to health services."[2]

---

2. UNHCR, "UN Experts," paras. 2–9.

STRUCTURAL CHANGE

There is a reason that these views that I have come to understand as truth are now being espoused by countries around the world. It is because, as humans, we are seeking to do better. We are all realizing that looking at substance use from a punitive lens is not effective, and more importantly, it is not accurate. It is my hope that through my firsthand frontline stories, you can now understand why the UN espouses these views. This is what it looks like when God is at work globally.

As Christians in a country in which a majority of citizens still call themselves Christian, we have a lot of say in our own nation's public policy. We represent many of the votes that can decide how we as a society should treat "the widows and orphans" among us. We have the privilege and the obligation to demand a more thoughtful approach from our elected officials. We can insist that scientific evidence plus the voices of people with lived experience be heard. We can proclaim the good news that the lives of people who use drugs are valuable and beautiful in the eyes of our Lord. And we can fight hard for those lives.

Interventions such as decriminalization, safer supply, and supervised consumption are expressions of radical love. This is the love that looks past the norms of society, questions harmful laws, and seeks to recognize and affirm the value of every person. It is a love that, in my personal and professional opinion, most closely follows the path of Jesus, and should be the way of those who sincerely call him Savior and Lord.

Conclusion

THE ROLE OF THE church is to proclaim and live out the good news to the world. I've written this book because I want you to know that the care of people who use drugs is a practice of good news. I can tell you that in tiny, tiny ways that are almost invisible to most, the kingdom of God is slowly being received into the lives of people who use drugs. But don't just take my word for it. Let me end this book by including a letter that was written to the editor of *Christian Week* in response to an article I wrote about my work at Insite.

> I was so touched by what I read. I am over two years clean and sober. I am from East Van. I was a regular client at Insite, and I was also at OnSite. I am so grateful for Insite and all the wonderful staff whom I call my angels. They saved my life. I don't live in Vancouver anymore. I live in Kelowna. I was very fortunate to get out while I could. Gratitude, compassion, and empathy are huge in my life today.
>
> It is so important to keep Insite open. I was one of the people who shot up using mud puddles in back alleys and shared needles. I am lucky to not be dead and I never felt like I belonged anywhere in life.
>
> *Jackie Douglas*
> *Kelowna, BC*[1]

---

1. Douglas, "Letter to the Editor."

CONCLUSION

If harm-reduction programs are shut down, the Jackie Douglases of the world will be remembered by obituaries instead of thoughtful letters to the editor. Without Christian advocacy for addiction medicine, even more people will die.

Throughout history, we can look back at the role of the church in ending slavery, in fighting apartheid, in caring for the lowest of the low. We can also see times when the church has perpetuated injustice, stolen children from their families, and turned a blind eye to those who are suffering. The question for each generation is what we choose to see, what we choose to struggle with. God always calls us to see people the way he sees them.

The main purpose of this book is that Christians will better understand the complexity of stories that each person with addiction brings to the table—and notice the way that God works among people with addiction. It is my hope that Christians will then recognize and defend the place of addiction care, including harm reduction, decriminalization, and public policy change, as bringing hope to people who use drugs by meeting them where they are at and treating their illnesses.

But my subversive hope is that hearing my journey will have caused you to deepen your own—by chatting with the homeless family that lives blocks from where you work, or seeing the person in the alley down the street as someone's beloved brother and a good person. When you start building relationships with people you would otherwise just walk past on the street, you are living out the love of God. Not only that, you are opening yourself up to receive blessings that knowing people with addiction might bring into your life. It's okay to not know how to get started—you just gotta ask for help and be willing to start somewhere. In this way, you will find the kingdom of God coming to earth all around you as more and more people are treated with dignity, respect, and compassion.

Bibliography

American Medical Association. "Treatment Versus Criminalization—Physician Role in Drug Addiction During Pregnancy H-420.970." American Medical Association, PolicyFinder, 2023. https://policysearch.ama-assn.org/policyfinder/detail/addiction%20pregnancy?uri=%2FAMADoc%2FHOD.xml-0-3713.xml.

American Psychiatric Association. "Substance-related and Addictive Disorders." In *Diagnostic and Statistical Manual of Mental Disorders*, 541. 5th ed. Text rev. Washington, DC: American Psychiatric Association, 2022.

Douglas, Jackie. "Letter to the Editor." ChristianWeek, October 14, 2010.

Felitti, Vincent, et al. "Relationship of Childhood Abuse and Household Dysfunction to Many of the Leading Causes of Death in Adults." *American Journal of Preventive Medicine* 14.4 (1998) 245–58.

Henry, Bonnie. "Stopping the Harm: Decriminalization of People Who Use Drugs in BC." Office of the Provincial Health Officer, Special Report, 2019. https://www2.gov.bc.ca/assets/gov/health/about-bc-s-health-care-system/office-of-the-provincial-health-officer/reports-publications/special-reports/stopping-the-harm-report.pdf.

"The Official Report of the Debates of the House of Commons of the Dominion of Canada." Third Session, Fifth Parliament, Vol XVIII. McLean, Rogers, and Co., 1885.

Perrin, Benjamin. *Overdose: Heartbreak and Hope in Canada's Opioid Crisis*. Toronto: Penguin Canada, 2022.

Taylor, Josephine, et al. "The Criminalisation of Miscarriage Associated with Illicit Substance Consumption Whilst Pregnant." *Medicine, Science, and the Law* 63 (2022) 260–61. https://www.ncbi.nlm.nih.gov/pmc/articles/PMC10262324/pdf/10.1177_00258024221140666.pdf.

UNHCR. "UN Experts Call for End to Global 'War on Drugs.'" UNHCR Press Release, June 23, 2023. https://www.ohchr.org/en/press-releases/2023/06/un-experts-call-end-global-war-drugs.

www.ingramcontent.com/pod-product-compliance
Lightning Source LLC
Chambersburg PA
CBHW031618170426
43195CB00037B/1079